TAEKWONDO

TAEKWONDO

Charles A. Stepan

THE LYONS PRESS

Guilford, Connecticut
An Imprint of The Globe Pequot Press

First Lyons Press edition 2002

Copyright © 2001 New Holland Publishers (UK) Ltd
Copyright © 2001 in text: Charles A. Stepan
Copyright © 2001 in illustrations:
New Holland Publishers (UK) Ltd
Copyright © 2002 in photographs: James Evans and Nicholas Aldridge
with the exception of the individual photographers and/or
their agents as listed on page 93.

First published by New Holland Publishers (UK) Ltd, 2001

ISBN 1 58574 448 4

2 4 6 8 10 9 7 5 3 1

Reproduction by Hirt & Carter (Cape) Pty Ltd
Printed and bound in Malaysia by Times Offset (M) Sdn Bhd

DISCLAIMER

The author and publishers have made every effort to ensure that the information contained in this book was accurate at the time of going to press, and accept no responsibility for any injury or inconvenience sustained by any person using this book or following the advice provided herein.

AUTHOR'S ACKNOWLEDGMENTS

Sam Naples for his help with some of the text;
James Evans for his photographic expertise;
as well as Karyn Richards, the Commissioning
Editor at New Holland Publishers, and the
Editor of this book, Lauren Copley, for their
tenacity. Lastly to Grandmaster Kae Bae Chun
— the foundation.

DEDICATION

For Bitsy . . . for everything.

CONTENTS

INTRODUCTION

Open the dojang door

Taekwondo is a Korean martial art. Though rooted in the karate of Japan, particularly Okinawa, the powerful kicking, slashing and spinning art of today bears little resemblance to the ground-rooted, reverse-punching techniques of the islands on which it originated. Despite its ancient roots, modern taekwondo has evolved primarily in Korea over the past 50 years. Discarding the old and less useful, martial arts experts redesigned it into what is currently one of the most promoted martial arts in the world.

Literally translated, taekwondo means 'foot-fist way.' The 'do' relates to the state of harmony with oneself. The principle is that when you have harmony within yourself, it is generally not difficult to be in harmony with nature and even with your adversaries.

Taekwondo aims to teach students how to develop their full human potential through tried and tested methods. This is combined with effective tools that reinforce this potential with courage and confidence. Through rigorous training, while using your feet and fists, you achieve a way of self-fulfilment.

The link with karate

The basic punches and kicks of modern taekwondo are the same as those used in karate. Many of karate's hand strikes and basic kicks are also used in taekwondo; the difference is in their presentation.

In karate, the vaunted reverse punch, front kick, side kick and reverse kick are devastating techniques when landed. In taekwondo these techniques have been developed and adapted to ensure that a student can overcome an opponent's speed and/or strength.

Taekwondo practitioners have mastered new ways to penetrate fighting defences by using stepping, hopping, jumping and flying techniques that have proven their effectiveness in international martial arts competitions, even when exponents of different fighting arts compete against each other in open tournaments.

One of the primary aims of this book is to introduce aspiring beginners to taekwondo and let them acquire reasonable proficiency in the hope that, one day, they too will be able to stand on the scratch mark (the starting position for a fight or match) of an international competition floor and not only survive but acquit themselves admirably.

While the purpose of martial arts training is to survive, learning to defend yourself effectively is another bonus of taekwondo training. Learning fighting skills, however, is not the ultimate purpose of taekwondo, it is only one of the aims of this martial art.

Together with self-defence, form practice and breaking, students study various fighting techniques. They then attempt to perfect their skills in order to understand human nature and, most importantly, to reach a better understanding of themselves. Apart from building physical ability and alertness, attaining greater self-control, speed, strength and agility, taekwondo is a means of bringing the body back into association with the mind.

A student's skills and path of self-mastery are honed under the scrutiny of a master. This takes weeks, months, and even years of sweat and practice. Technique is emphasized through repetition until it becomes instinctive. Through discipline and ongoing encouragement the spirit is developed.

Students are tested by being placed in stressful combat situations at their own level with no-one to rely on but themselves and their art. To 'fail' does not mean you fail your school or fellow students, but shows that you have failed yourself. By placing demands on themselves, students are able to build their willpower and increase their own sense of accomplishment.

opposite THE BELT YOU WEAR SIGNIFIES HOW FAR YOU HAVE COME AND HOW FAR YOU HAVE YET TO GO.

MANY TAEKWONDO HISTORIANS BELIEVE THAT THEIR MARTIAL ART WAS SECRETLY PRESERVED BY THE MONKS OF BUDDHIST TEMPLES LIKE THIS ONE, THE BUPJU-SA (ALSO CALLED POPJU-SA), DURING KOREA'S TURBULENT PAST.

Return to the roots

Korea's ancient and modern martial arts history would be sufficiently complicated to follow even if all Korean martial artists were in agreement, which is not the case. Pride, both personal and national, combined with a great proliferation of taekwondo styles, has muddied the water to a large degree.

A comprehensive study is required to accurately trace taekwondo's progress from its ancient origins to its present status. Korea's ancient martial arts roots encompass various disciplines. These include Taekyon; Kongsudo (empty hands); Tangsudo (Tang-dynasty empty-hands way); Taesudo (kick-fist way); Kwan Bup (Quanfa, Kenpo, or Chinese Boxing); Tangsu (Tang hand); Subak (striking hands), and Chabi (Taiken — a combination of Kenpo and Jujutsu, a Japanese art of leverage, throwing and choking).

Many present-day Korean martial arts still use these names, but only Taekyon — a seldom-practised kicking art — has a recorded lineage that can be traced back to its original roots. Other modern disciplines such as Subak or Tangsudo have a legendary connection to the arts of today — they use the ancient name, but have no provable lineage.

Tracing taekwondo's modern history

Taekwondo's modern history goes back only about 55 years to the end of World War II.

The year 1904 was a sad time in Korea's history as the Japanese began their westward expansion into Korea. By 1910 Japanese forces had effectively occupied the country and one of their goals was to suppress Korean heritage and culture. Any martial arts that were being practised in Korea at the time were banned on pain of death.

As the pace of conflict began to intensify and events moved closer to World War II, many young Korean men were forced to cooperate with the Japanese armed forces by having to become soldiers or labourers. Many of those subjugated had an opportunity first to observe and later to participate in Japanese karate classes (it is now known that most of them studied either the Shotokan or Shudokan style).

The first Korean-taught martial arts school surfaced in the city of Kaisông (previously called Songdo, Korea's ancient capital) in the last year of World War II.

Pioneers of the art

Byung Jik Ro, who was to play a key role in the growth of Korean martial arts, ran the very first school. Won Kook Lee and Il Sup Chun followed a short time later by opening a second one in Seoul. When the war ended these pioneer schools were forced to close their doors, but they reopened in 1946 and it was not long before several more had been established throughout Korea.

Just as these schools started regaining their tenuous foothold, they again had to close — a few years later — when the Korean War broke out in 1950.

In 1953 peace had returned to the war-ravaged region and the founding schools (known as *kwans*) began to resume. Korean martial artists also initiated attempts to unify the different branches by establishing the Korean Kong Soo Do (empty hands) Association.

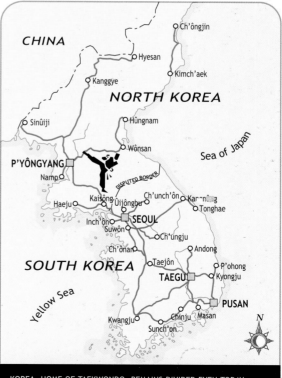

KOREA, HOME OF TAEKWONDO, REMAINS DIVIDED EVEN TODAY.

Sadly, dissension soon set in and the association was dissolved. As the *kwans* continued to grow and multiply, techniques and training methods were refined and redesigned, adding greatly to the richness of what is now known as taekwondo.

New styles emerge

With the emergence of several new schools and styles of the art, *kwan* leaders again called a meeting in 1955. Called the Taesudo-Kongsudo Conference, the aim of this meeting was to achieve unity and it is believed that the name taekwondo was first proposed here. In the years that followed, the organization underwent numerous changes as the country was hit by tremendous political upheaval in 1961.

DEDICATED TRAINING HONES THE BODY INTO A LETHAL WEAPON.

The Korean Taekwondo Association finally received official acceptance from the Korean Amateur Sports Association in 1964.

With time, taekwondo gained increasing recognition as an effective martial art and spread across Asia and further afield to several other countries including the United States, Canada, West Germany, Italy, Turkey and the United Arab Emirates.

Major organizations

There are currently only two major organizations that represent the interests of this martial art worldwide: the World Taekwondo Association (WTF) and the International Taekwondo Federation (ITF). Both sports organizations have the power to grant rank to practitioners who are recommended, but not necessarily known to them.

In contrast, the more traditional *kwan* schools grant rank only to those taekwondo students whom they have personally taught and tested.

In South Korea today, all taekwondo practitioners are graduates promoted by the World Taekwondo Federation, which is the official national system of South Korea. They practise what most of the rest of the world deems to be a sport.

Although old-style *kwan* schools are not allowed in modern-day Korea, the traditional *kwan* system continues to flourish worldwide. Many who cling faithfully to their *kwan* roots practise their sport in competition, while their martial arts techniques, handed down through original *kwans*, is also much in evidence on the training floors of *dojangs* around the globe.

'Achieve your purpose but properly stop, and never venture to rely upon your strength;
Achieve your purpose but never parade your success;
Achieve your purpose but never boast of your ability;
Achieve your purpose but only as an unavoidable step;
Achieve your purpose but never show off your strength;
For things age and decay after they reach their prime;
Whatever is against Tao soon ceases to be.'

Lao Tzu (Chinese philosopher, born 604BC)

Entering the *dojang*

If you have driven past a taekwondo studio and wondered what goes on behind the doors, it is time you stopped to find out why this is one of the fastest growing martial arts in the world.

You will probably find that the *dojang* — the Korean term for a taekwondo studio — is an uncluttered, clean and well-used area. Some *dojang* floors are wooden or carpeted and some have loose mats, but all should be spotless. In essence, the *dojang* is really a reflection of the students who train there. Mirrors line at least one of the walls and are meant to be functional: they serve as additional instructors, reflecting incorrect stance and improper displays of hand- or footwork. The mirrors also show the encouraging results of hard work as students strive to improve their techniques.

One or two kicking bags are likely to be hanging from the ceiling, accompanied by a row of kicking and punching bags along the wall. Teachers use these training tools to encourage proper technique.

Flags will be found hanging on the *dojang* wall — one will honour your home country, while another will honour Korea, taekwondo's original home.

Bowing shows respect

If you find yourself in the studio during a taekwondo session you will notice that the students bow to the flags and to the instructor as they step on and off the *dojang* floor. This gesture is a sign of respect for their country, their art and their teacher. Mostly, it is a sign of respect for their own personal battlefield where they have learnt to challenge, and conquer their fears.

Learning the art of taekwondo is a long journey; the way of this art focuses not on the abilities learnt, but rather on providing the pathway to learn and teach them. Regardless of whether your martial arts school is affiliated to the ITF, WTF, or *kwan* system, this book aims to ensure that beginners learn pure taekwondo rather than one of the many cross-training arts that are available. Just one example of this is Taebo, a popular combination of aerobics and taekwondo. Although classes are frequently presented by martial arts teachers, students mistakenly believe that they are being taught an actual 'fighting art'.

This manual will highlight basic training techniques, discuss objectives and philosophy and focus on the practical application of taekwondo in self-defence.

BOWING NOT ONLY SIGNIFIES RESPECT TO YOUR OPPONENT AND YOUR ART, BUT REMINDS YOU OF THE RESPONSIBILITY YOU HAVE WHEN YOU ARE USING THE POTENTIALLY DANGEROUS TECHNIQUES YOU HAVE BEEN TAUGHT.

STARTING OUT

Basics and dojang etiquette

All martial artists must learn technique. Every master and every instructor has a method he or she deems best to teach students this technique. When you have learnt all the techniques and forms taught by your particular school, know every rule and tenet of your school's style and have passed your tests at each *gup* level (*gup* is the Korean word for step), you may be invited to test for a black belt. Not all black-belt practitioners are the same. It is quite commonly observed that black-belt students vary not only in physical skills, but also in the martial arts knowledge they display.

All masters are willing to teach you the technique of their style, but there is more to taekwondo than simply mastering style. Some of the older masters possess special knowledge that they impart only to those students who demonstrate that they really want to learn and deserve it. These students are willing to go the extra mile in proving to their master that they are worthy of going along the 'way of taekwondo'.

Most of the old masters imparted their knowledge to high-ranked students they regarded as being worthy. Many of these, in turn, became masters themselves and honoured junior instructors placed under them by passing on their understanding of the way of taekwondo. This 'way' is the pathway to which the 'do' in the word taekwondo refers.

The right teacher

It makes sense that at the start you should select a teacher you feel confident will be able to teach you what you need to learn. In return, you should have no reservations in giving your commitment to the master or one of his hand-picked instructors.

When selecting a teacher, the framed certificates displayed on a *dojang* wall are not necessarily an accurate indication of qualifications achieved. Also, bear in mind that in the martial arts world such certificates usually only take you back one generation. A martial arts 'generation' is not equivalent to the usual understanding of the word: an art or style is founded by one person whose students subsequently become the first generation. The students they teach then become the second generation, and so on.

You're on the right track if you walk into a *dojang* that is recognized by the national governing body of the country in which you live. If a school doesn't fit this picture, enquire about the martial arts lineage and background of the instructor. If his rank is lower than a fourth-degree black belt, then his studio and brochures should indicate that his teaching has been sanctioned by a higher-ranked instructor.

Many, if not most, traditional instructors above the rank of fourth degree still honour their teacher in their brochures. When a prospective school accredits its training programme to an honoured grand master it is likely to have a solid foundation.

For the raw beginner, observing a taekwondo class is usually not very helpful (especially if your martial arts knowledge is limited to films or television programmes) unless you possess previous martial arts training. Martial arts schools abound with teachers who hold black-belt qualifications, but have branched off after attaining this rank to impart their personal brand of training. In taekwondo, holders of black belts are not looked up to in awe — they are rather viewed as serious students. A black belt should not be seen as a magical endowment — it is simply another step along 'the way'.

Today, it is not that easy to find a taekwondo school headed by an honoured oriental grand master. For the most part, however, martial arts teachers are likely to

be legitimate black belt instructors, since frauds or poor teachers will usually have a bad reputation that is not easily shed.

A convenient way to select a taekwondo school is to consult your local telephone directory or yellow pages. Alternatively you could try your national or regional governing body. Once you have located a grand master or instructor, make enquiries and gather information about the school you consider joining. In general, higher ranked masters are easy to talk to and will be honoured by your call, so heed their advice. It is important to find a good school because if you have to leave it for any reason, any training you may already have undergone will not have been wasted.

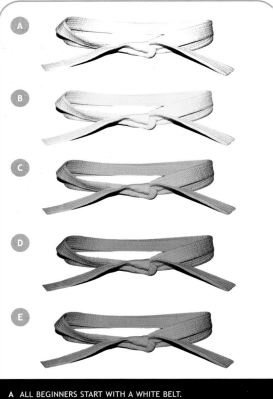

A ALL BEGINNERS START WITH A WHITE BELT.

B A YELLOW BELT USUALLY FOLLOWS THE WHITE BELT; SOME SCHOOLS MAY FOLLOW THAT WITH AN ORANGE LEVEL.

C A GREEN BELT IS ACHIEVED IN TWO STAGES, LIKE THE BLUE BELT.

D THE BLUE BELT CONSISTS OF TWO STAGES, 'LOW' AND 'HIGH'.

E THE BROWN-BELT STAGE IS TWICE AS LONG AS THE OTHER LEVELS.

Progressing through training

All taekwondo schools operate on a *gup* or step system. The use of coloured belts, which denote *gup* levels, is designed to let your instructors know what level of training you have already reached, as they may be training hundreds of students. The belt system is also used as an incentive for the student to advance to the next step or level of training. Most *gup* steps are based on a range of one to ten, with ten indicating a white-belt beginner and one being a high brown belt, ready to test for his black belt.

The description of the belt levels is based on the assumption that a student attends an average of three classes a week. This general description cannot be applied universally as each training school sets its own training regimen and belt designations.

In taekwondo, belt ratings usually start with a white-belt beginner stage and then progress to yellow. In most cases, reaching the yellow-belt level would entail a three-month training period, followed by a further three months of training once a student has been tested on this level and passed it. The next step is the green belt, consisting of a 'low' and a 'high' ranking. Each requires about three months of training.

School owners do not follow the same system, however, and there is no standard rule of thumb in the belt levels offered. For example, the same colour green belt may be worn in several schools, but the teaching will be more advanced for high green belts. In other schools, a taped stripe may be added to the belt to distinguish the difference between a low and a high ranking.

There is a test at each level. Once a student has graduated to a high green belt, he or she moves on to another two-stage step — the blue belt, which also entails three-month training periods for each stage. The brown belt follows this, although some Korean schools use a red belt to denote this level.

As with the two previous levels, a brown (or red) belt consists of two stages. The difference is that the training periods for this advanced ranking are six months at each level. Once brown-level students have trained for a year, they go on to spend another year as a black-belt-in-training.

After following this programme for a period of around 3½ years, training three times a week and passing all the tests at each level — they may be considered for black-belt ranking. Other factors also play a role in an instructor's decision whether to promote a student to black-belt rank or not. These include the student's attitude, performance ability and, sometimes, outstanding character or lack thereof.

Some schools may add an orange belt (usually after the yellow level) and a purple belt after the blue belt level. In addition, other *dojangs* add stripes to a student's belt (usually taped at the belt ends), that signify advanced achievements at the particular belt level.

Dojang etiquette

An important concept the beginner should grasp at the outset is that taekwondo is not just an exercise class. The training also focuses on teaching techniques for use in intimidating and dangerous situations where you may be confronted by someone with a weapon or a person who wants to hurt or even kill you.

Why rules are important

The reinforcement of rigid rules through repetitive actions may seem tedious to students, but is necessary. If a certain rule requires you to swing your head and look before you turn, constant repetition will teach you to do so without thinking. Some rules, although they may seem harsh, help to encourage a proper and receptive attitude while also promoting discipline and uniformity among students.

General rules

■ Shoes are forbidden on the work-out floor, with the exception of soft-soled martial arts shoes for which the student must gain prior permission from the school's owner. (These shoes have thin, treadless soles and can be purchased from martial arts outlet stores or through martial arts publications.)

■ Most schools will only allow such soft shoes to be worn by students who suffer from particular medical conditions such as diabetes, which requires special attention to the care of the feet.

■ Smoking and chewing gum, eating and drinking are forbidden in the studio.

■ A student who arrives late for a class must ask permission from the instructor to join in the class.

■ An instructor's word is never questioned.

■ On the training floor, a student only speaks when responding to or asking a question of the instructor.

■ Instructors are addressed as Sir if male and Ma'am if female, or just *Saw bawm*.

■ Students should bow before addressing their instructor.

■ During classes, students should refrain from laughing or talking socially with other students, they must pay attention to their instructors.

■ Jewellery (i.e. rings, bracelets and necklaces) should never be worn on the work-out floor. They can cause injury to the wearer or another student, i.e. by getting hit with a ring or bracelet, or getting choked by one's own necklace.

■ A beginner student must not attempt to teach others outside the *dojang*.

■ Students should only use the self-defence techniques they learn as a means of defending themselves or members of their family.

■ Taekwondo students are expected to display good manners, always be conscious of the fact that they represent their training school, and conduct themselves appropriately at all times.

TAEKWONDO IS CUSTOMARILY PRACTISED BAREFOOT. IF YOU NEED TO PROTECT YOUR FEET, GET PROPER FOOTWEAR.

DOJANGS DISPLAY TWO FLAGS: ONE HONOURING KOREA AND THE OTHER THE SCHOOL'S NATIVE COUNTRY.

Personal behaviour in the *dojang*

■ It is a customary sign of respect to bow when entering or leaving the *dojang*, and when stepping onto or off the work-out floor.

■ When entering or leaving the studio, bow toward the flags. If the school's master instructor is on the floor, you would first bow toward the flags before bowing to the master.

■ When you are talking to your master, show your respect by not crossing your arms but keep them relaxed at your sides.

■ Keep your toe- and fingernails clean as well as neatly trimmed.

■ Pay attention to your instructor and speak only when necessary.

■ If you arrive late, put on your uniform (*dobok*) and wait behind the class until it is convenient to ask the instructor's permission to join.

■ Always maintain body discipline — stand and sit erect with a straight back. Avoid slouching.

■ Do not sit unless you are asked to do so and never lie down on the floor unless it is part of a class demonstration. When sitting, cross your legs and do not lean against anything.

■ If you must leave the *dojang* area or work-out floor, ask your instructor if you may be excused.

■ Smokers may only smoke outside and are expected to leave the *dojang* to do so.

■ Avoid profanity as it is a sign of anger and shows poor self-control.

■ Never spar without first getting permission from your instructor.

■ Always aim to maintain an atmosphere of mutual respect, care and goodwill.

Safety rules

Horseplay is not appropriate in any area of the dojang. Safety should always be an integral part of taekwondo training. The following rules ensure that training is effective and safe:

■ Always remain careful and alert, especially in the work-out areas where students are punching, kicking and leaping through the air.

■ Taekwondo techniques can maim and injure others — ensure that you practise with concentration and deadly seriousness and always keep your eyes on your opponent.

■ While sparring, try to maintain the safety zone you have been taught.

■ Never deliberately strike anyone with the intent to injure or do bodily harm.

■ Think before you move and move wisely.

■ Refrain from discussing or debating any aspects of your taekwondo training with outsiders. Also, avoid demonstrating taekwondo manoeuvres or techniques you may have learned to other people without first having obtained your master's permission. This last point is especially important, because unsupervised demonstrations could endanger others and compromise your personal safety.

Taekwondo gear

The *dobok*, taekwondo's traditional uniform, still resembles the white *dogi* uniform used in karate (except for members of the World Taekwondo Federation, whose *dobok* top is described below). The loose cotton uniform is similar to the everyday clothing worn by nearly every Korean in the past.

In days gone by, the colour white was seen as a sign of purity. White clothing was worn by rich and poor alike to eliminate class distinction. Both men and women wore the simple wide-legged cotton pants and jacket top which provided comfort and complete freedom of movement. Although white is the colour of the original taekwondo uniform it is not unusual, today, to find *doboks* in a variety of colours, sometimes even in mix-and-match colour combinations.

A modern version

The World Taekwondo Federation, nationally sponsored representative of the art that is currently practised in Korea, has introduced a new type of *dobok*. While still traditionally white, the *dobok* jacket no longer features the slant-cut front opening. It is probably more correct to describe the new-version jacket with its closed front as a blouse, as the garment is simply pulled over the head like a conventional sweatshirt.

The *kwan* schools and the International Taekwondo Federation still favour the traditional white *dobok* uniform which has a front slant-cut jacket.

The jacket is worn with the left flap over the top of the right flap. These uniforms also have side ties that may be used, but are often ignored by taekwondo practitioners as experience has shown that the ties often get torn out of the stitching.

Ladies wearing this type of jacket top usually wear a T-shirt type of garment underneath. The more fashion-conscious may even ensure that this T-shirt matches the colour of their belts.

Patches are often stitched onto the jacket. The school's patch is usually placed over the left breast, while flags may be placed on the top of the arms in most schools. However, the use and placement of patches and flags on a taekwondo uniform must be under the direction of your master instructor. As with the older-style garment, patches, flags or logos can be stitched directly onto the blouse, although nowadays it is more likely that the school's logo has already been screened-printed onto the fabric.

Whatever type of uniform your school requires you to wear, it is important to note that once you are in possession of your *dobok*, no other clothing may be worn during class training sessions.

Be aware also that instructors frown upon students who fail to prepare themselves and their uniforms for classes. Always ensure that your *dobok* is clean and without any wrinkles or tears. A sloppily dressed student is generally viewed as one who lacks the forethought that is necessary to learn the serious business of a martial art.

THE MODERN *DOBOK* FEATURES A TOP WITH A V-NECK OPENING THAT IS SIMPLY PULLED OVER THE HEAD.

Useful terminology

Since taekwondo is represented worldwide, it is only sensible that the language which is used during training classes be universally taught in terms that any students travelling from one country to another can understand. Given its Korean foundation, Korean is the obvious language of choice. You do not have to learn the entire Korean language, only the appropriate terms for your training sessions.

Schools do, however, use their own language along with Korean. In the United States, for example, classes are taught in English along with the appropriate Korean phrases and descriptions. In some parts of Canada classes are often taught in English, Korean and French.

Most training drills (hands-on fighting, self-defence or conditioning) taught during a taekwondo class require all of the students to be at the same level of training. Each step in the drill is numbered, the movements are executed in sequence, and the instructor will probably count them out in Korean.

For that reason, it is very helpful to learn how to count in the Korean language. Note that Korean words with more than one syllable are pronounced by placing the accent or emphasis on the first syllable.

Counting in Korean

ENGLISH	PHONETIC KOREAN	
One	Hana	(pronounced Hawna)
Two	Dul	
Three	Set	
Four	Net	
Five	Da sat	(pronounced Daw set)
Six	Ya sat	(pronounced Yah set)
Seven	Il goop	
Eight	Ya dul	(pronounced Yaw dul)
Nine	Ah hool	
Ten	Yul	

Numbers after 10 are counted Ten-one, Ten-two, etc. Therefore, the number 11 would be *Yul-hana*; 12 would be *Yul-dul*, 13 is *Yul-set*, and so on down the line to number 19, which would be *Yul-ah hool*, with 20 being *Soo mool*. Counting higher than 20 follows in the same way: *Soo mool-hana* (21), *Soo mool-dul* (22), *Soo mool-set* (23). It sounds more difficult than it really is. Also, learning to count up to 30 should be sufficient for any taekwondo class.

A BASIC VOCABULARY OF KOREAN WORDS ENABLES STUDENTS TO FOLLOW INSTRUCTIONS AND COUNT ALONG WITH AN INSTRUCTOR.

Useful terms

It will be easier to follow instructions and get a more accurate feel for the art if you come to grips with some basic Korean words. Here are some of the most important ones you should learn:

ENGLISH	PHONETIC KOREAN
Instructor	Saw bawm nim
School/studio	Dojang
Uniform	Dobok
Form	Hyung
Self-defence	Ho shin sul
Free spar (as command)	Cha yoo tae ryun
Breaking	Kyuk paw
Fighting stance	Tae ryun chaw sawge
Ready (ready stance)	Jun be
Begin	Si jawk
End	Ko mawn
Continue	Kae sok
Attention	Cha ryot
Horse stance	Chaw choom sawge
Yell or shout	Ki yap
Turn	Toe ra
Turn around	Ti ro toe ra
Turn right	U yang u
Turn left	Cha yang cha
Black belt (the belt)	Hook de
Black belt (the person)	Yoo dan jaw

Be careful when using the Korean language as there are at least three different ways to say anything. Respect is important in the Korean culture and proper respect must also be shown in your speech. Different phrasing is used for varying stations of social honour: one for those on a higher social level than you consider yourself, one for those on an equal level, and one for those you regard as socially inferior to you. In this way, if you were asking someone to come to you, the literal translations of the three forms of speech would be:

'Would you please come here?' (Idiwah ship she o)

'Would you come here?' (Idiwah she o)

'Get over here!' (Idiwah)

Words for basic manoeuvres

Apart from general terminology, it is helpful to learn the Korean words for some basic manoeuvres you'll be using during training on a regular basis:

Hand techniques

ENGLISH	PHONETIC KOREAN
Medium punch	Jung dawn chi lu ki
Low block	Ha dawn mawki
Inside block	Cho noki
Outside block	Cho nayki
High block	Song dawn mawki
High punch	Song dawn chi lu ki
Spear hand	Kwan soo
Chop	Soo do chigi
Side punch	Yup chi lu ki
Cat-stance block	Kwang e sae mawki
Ridge hand	Paah do

Kicking techniques

ENGLISH	PHONETIC KOREAN
Front kick	Ap chaggi
Front thrust kick	Ap ki pun chaggi
Side kick	Yup chaggi
Roundhouse kick	Tol yoh chaggi
Back kick	Tui chaggi
Reverse kick	Tui tol yoh chaggi

Optional conversational terms

ENGLISH	PHONETIC KOREAN
Hello	Ahn yung haw shim neekah
Thank you	Comb sum needah
I'm sorry	Mi ahn ham needah
I am fine	Jo sum needah
Excuse me	Sil lae ham needah
Goodbye (1st person)	Ahn yung e kay ship she o
Goodbye (2nd person)	Ahn yung e kaw ship she o

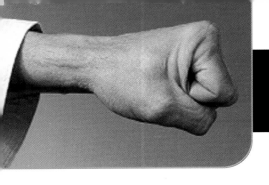

LEARNING THE BASICS

As a new taekwondo student you will start by learning basic footwork and then move on to learn simple blocking and striking techniques using both your hands and feet. During these initial classes, conditioning and stretching play a great part and they will continue to do so throughout your taekwondo training.

Once you begin to feel familiar with the training routine and can kick and punch with some dexterity you will be taught how to move with controlled balance. Then you learn how to adjust your distance when facing an opponent (who is no more adept at attempting these new skills than you are at this early stage). The next step is for your instructor to help you coordinate all of the above and to encourage your efforts with kindly correction and praise.

Trying your hand at sparring

Once the basics have been conquered students are introduced to sparring. During these sessions the instructor will involve other students who are at the same training skill level. On occasion, instructors themselves may spar with students and allow them to hit into openings they purposefully create during the session. These mandatory practice sparring rounds help to instill confidence in the 'new warriors'.

When you take part in a sparring session you will be patiently corrected, carefully supervised, studied and evaluated until the instructor believes you are ready to try your hand at a more realistic version of taekwondo combat. From there on you can expect the hitting to become quite a bit harder as the training increases in pace and intensity.

Coping with pressure

At this stage of training, instructors may choose to reveal another, less pleasant, side to their personality by urging, jeering, sneering and at times maybe even insulting you, the student. The aim is not to intimidate, but rather to coerce you to use all your skill and ability to cope with the pressure normally found in a combat situation. So, don't feel insulted if your instructor sweeps your feet out from under you to teach you respect for stance and distance. A quick shot to the solar plexus may cause you to gasp for air while you think about defending yourself more adequately, and a lack of respect or a lapse of manners might result in you having to perform knuckle push-ups.

Rejoice if you have this type of instructor, who is of the 'old' martial arts school and has your best interests at heart. By ridding you of the misguided notion that taekwondo is fun and games, a tough instructor is actually doing you a favour.

If this glimpse into training sounds alarming, bear in mind that taekwondo is *meant* to be intimidating. This martial art should be taken seriously and, from the start, students will learn that training is geared towards letting them know what they can look forward to. Not surprisingly, this stage of training presents a watershed: some students choose to continue, while others decide that the taekwondo regimen is not for them.

The instructor is the obvious key to any student's future. If a student is discouraged or even a little frightened at this stage he may hesitate to go further. In that case the instructor only loses a student, but the student loses an opportunity to undergo a wonderful transformation that will affect the rest of his or her life. This opportunity teaches the student how to use training tools such as fighting to handle pressure when placed in stressful situations. When students learn to fight well and wisely, they get to know their abilities and do not feel the need to prove themselves when

opposite DEDICATED PRACTICE AND DETERMINATION ARE ULTIMATELY REWARDED WITH BLACK-BELT STATUS.

their pride is challenged. Taekwondo equips you with the confidence and skill to handle a variety of situations — both in the *dojang* and in everyday life.

The transformation begins with novice students — they are driven harder to please, and by pleasing their instructor they learn proper technique. Later, the rapport between student and instructor, together with the intensity of the training and combat sessions, will help to channel the state of aggression into which the instructor has goaded the student.

Under careful guidance, a student's aggressiveness is funnelled into a creativity that heightens everything he does. In the heat of combat this creativity teaches the student to be where he wants to be, when he wants to be there, and where his opponent does not expect him. He learns to rely upon an innate radar-like skill until he blocks and fights with an instinctive calmness of mind and with a confidence that belies his lack of skill.

The protective sponge- and rubber-filled padding worn up till now is removed as each student discovers that thumps and bruises can be avoided simply by skillfully moving out of the way.

PROTECTIVE HELMET, VEST PROTECTOR, GLOVES AND FOOT PADS ARE NEEDED FOR INTER-SCHOOL COMPETITIONS.

The improved skill becomes evident in effective blocking, side-stepping, slipping and ducking. As students face the array of opponents that are placed before them, they start to realize that they are now able to take advantage of others' errors. With the guidance of their instructors, they press on, honing their new skills through work and sweat until they have refined everything they have been taught.

Students learn more effective new fighting skills that are subsequently discarded and replaced with superior techniques. Above all, they find that they now possess the instinctive ability to react spontaneously under pressure. They are now able to respond almost automatically with techniques that are appropriate to the threat they are facing.

All the while, students are absorbing lessons in respect, fairness, self-control and confidence. As they grow and change, they learn to look into the hearts and souls of their fellow students, watching how they, too, are growing and learning.

The dedication and time a student spends learning and training is rewarded by advancing rank and the slow but sure progress toward the coveted black belt. However, even once this goal is achieved there is still much to learn. A black belt is still only a stepping stone along a long, hard way.

If one has taken in the lessons learnt on the *dojang* floor, the honour of being included in the select group of black-belt holders will be accepted with humility. It is an overwhelming experience and will make one vow to work even harder.

With the acceptance as a 'serious student' another inner transformation occurs. The new black-belt holder will experience a sense of peace and a feeling of being more in control of mind and body. This powerful feeling will remain, even though the process of learning can never be complete.

Your first class

Not all beginners' classes are handled the same way. In the past, traditional studios tended to offer classes that were open to everyone, with students being able to choose attendance times.

STRETCHING EXERCISES ARE AN IMPORTANT WARM-UP ROUTINE.

Classes would typically begin with some stretching exercises and warm-up drills. Students would then be sent to certain areas of the work-out floor to join others of the same rank. There, an instructor would be assigned to teach only that group separately and apart from the rest of the class.

Nowadays, some taekwondo schools offer initial one-on-one introductory lessons, whereafter students are placed in classes right for their level, regardless of age. Others prefer to teach adults and children separately. Most modern studios have specified class schedules to ensure that all students with the same colour belts train together.

In most taekwondo classes, supervision is generally so good that injuries are very rare. If you see students sporting casts, bandages or bruises, their injuries are more likely to have been sustained during a heated game of football, baseball, hockey, basketball or other contact sport.

Despite initial apprehensions, students who choose a reputable instructor or master can always rest assured that they will not be expected or asked to do anything they are not capable of.

Stretching and warming up

Once you leave the dressing room to begin your first class you should bow toward the *dojang* flags before stepping onto the work-out area. If the master is on the floor, a bow should be directed toward him too.

When the class is called to order, take your place in the last line along with other white belts or beginners. The class will collectively bow to flags posted in the studio, and then to the instructor directing the class.

The first portion of the class is led by the instructor or an advanced student and involves all participants in stretching exercises. These may take 10–15 minutes; in some schools they could take as long as 30 minutes. Immediately after or during the stretching, loosening-up exercises or techniques are taught and practised by all the students.

Regardless of the various stretches or drills you are put through, remember that a taekwondo practitioner regards hamstring stretching exercises as the most important stretching drill.

A good warm-up and stretching session will help to prevent injury or strains to your muscles. However, whatever kicking you are practising — and taekwondo is primarily a kicking art — be aware that the leg you are kicking with hardly needs to be stretched. It is the leg that remains on the ground, the one you are standing on, which is doing the real stretching, hence the importance of hamstring exercises.

The stretching routines are usually followed by a series of warm-up drills that involve much punching and kicking. It is wise for beginners to closely watch their instructor, or students with higher-colour belts. Much can be learned by observing how experienced students demonstrate their techniques.

Unless you are in a class where all your fellow students have the same rank, the instructor will divide the class into differently ranked groups. This is where beginners start to learn the basic stances, blocks, punches and kicks.

Later, you will be introduced to form practice, as well as sparring and breaking. As a beginner, you have many things to learn, so pay close attention and get your money's worth.

A SITTING STRETCH: FROM A SITTING POSITION, BEND ONE LEG INWARD, REACH FORWARD OVER YOUR OUTSTRETCHED LEG AND HOLD YOUR TOES.

B INNER-THIGH STRETCH: SITTING ON BOTH BUTTOCKS, HOLD YOUR TOES AND BREATHE IN DEEPLY. AS YOU EXHALE, PRESS YOUR KNEES TOWARD THE FLOOR. YOU COULD ALSO BEND YOUR BACK AND TRY TO TOUCH THE FLOOR WITH YOUR HEAD.

C ALL-FOURS: PLACE YOUR FEET AS WIDE APART AS POSSIBLE, KEEPING THE SOLES FLAT ON THE FLOOR. WITH BACK STRAIGHT, PLACE PALMS FLAT ON THE FLOOR.

D SHOULDER STRETCH 1: BRING YOUR ARM ACROSS THE FRONT OF YOUR BODY AND PLACE IT IN THE BEND OF THE OTHER ARM.

E SHOULDER STRETCH 2: STRETCH YOUR ARMS OUT BEHIND YOU AND CLASP YOUR HANDS. LIFT THE ARMS WITHOUT BENDING FORWARD.

Essential know-how

Tying your belt

Hopefully, you are going to be tying your belt around you many, many times in the future, so it is important that you learn to do it correctly. This easy method is the one that is most commonly used:

A Find the middle of your belt, straighten it and hold it out in front of you with both hands at about waist height, letting the two equally long ends hang to the floor. Slide your hands approximately 45cm (17in) apart and hold the belt up against your stomach. Wrap it around your middle, crossing it in the small of your back and pulling the two ends back in front of you.

B Loop the right end under the double-wrapped belt to the left of centre (cross the ends again, left over right, holding them in place with your left hand).

C With your right hand, reach into the opening you have created by crossing over the end pieces and grab the belt end on the right to pull it back through the opening where your left hand is situated.

D Pull the ends of the belt tight around your middle section. Ensure that the right belt end is on the top and adjust the ends so that they are equal in length.

Tip: A quick way to check whether you have tied your belt correctly is to look down at the knot. The open slotted end of the belt should be on your left. With practice and some adjustments you will soon be able to tie your belt correctly in no time.

Making a proper fist

Making a proper fist is vital to prevent injury to your wrist and hand. Practise it many times, until it finally becomes second nature.

A Fold your fingertips over until they touch the padded area at the base of your fingers. Next roll the fingertips tightly into the palm of the hand and fold your thumb over them, downward.

B The two top knuckles, i.e. those of the index and middle fingers, are the hitting or contact surfaces.

Hand-wrist position for chopping techniques

An open fist is the proper alignment of hand and wrist for a correctly executed chop.

C Holding your hand palm downward straight out to your side, horizontally to the floor, make a fist. The normal rise of your knuckles above the extended wrist is the proper position of the fist, i.e. do not change the fist position by cocking the fist upward or downward. Keeping your arm extended, now open your fist and tuck your thumb underneath your palm. Using your left hand, push down at your elbow joint so that your fingertips point upward.

A fistful of useful hints

- To establish the contact surface of your fist: get into a push-up position while supporting yourself with the top two contact knuckles (*see* B). Letting your buttocks sag, hold this position for 30 seconds before getting up. The sensation you feel on your knuckles indicates the hitting portion of your fist.

- Your strike should never impact on the knuckles of your ring and little fingers, because you could sustain what is commonly known as 'boxer's fracture'. This painful injury affects the bone that runs along the outer edge of the hand, from the little finger knuckle to the wrist bone.

- The proper blocking technique is accomplished by bending the arm at the elbow joint. Hand and forearm should be in straight alignment.

- When chopping, note that the arm will extend and straighten with the pad roughly 0.5cm (2in) to the rear of the little finger as the impact area.

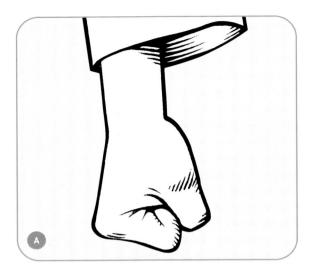

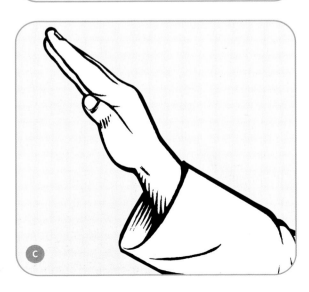

Focus — get vocal

Yell is a poor word to describe the martial arts 'Ki yap', a concentrated outburst of vocal energy. Shout, cry, scream — none of these verbs really describe this important martial arts element that constitutes focus. It is, perhaps, more accurate to describe the Ki yap as a 'barking' sound.

As a martial artist strikes, he exhales breath in an explosive Ki yap to concentrate his physical output on the intended target. When done correctly, the Ki yap will sound like 'EEE-YAHHHH'; the 'EEE' part of the Ki yap coinciding with the moment in which you initiate the strike, punch or kick. When you do this, inhale and tighten your midsection area to protect yourself from a quick counter.

When you exhale, sound the 'YAHHH' portion of the Ki yap at the same time, while concentrating all your force and focus on the selected target area. In a self-defence situation, a loud, forceful Ki yap from you may take the attacker completely unawares and momentarily confuse him, which will give you a brief advantage and allow you to make your escape.

WHEN USED PROPERLY, THE KI YAP HELPS TO FOCUS YOUR MIND AND PHYSICAL ENERGY.

T AEKWONDO'S TOOLS

Taekwondo was originally a 'no-touch' martial art, with great skill being acquired by mastering superb control in hand and foot strikes. Power was demonstrated through breaking exercises.

Today, protective sponge-like pads must be worn on the hands and feet in open competitions— a regulation that was brought about largely by insurance companies. In the United States, the increasing fear of unjustified lawsuits (and subsequent legal action) has had quite a significant impact on martial arts training, more so than in the rest of the world. Protective pads have now become compulsory gear in most open taekwondo competitions and during training sessions.

Need for protection

Originally, the purpose of introducing protective pads was to make competition fighting even safer, but there was a downside: they diminished the control skills of the taekwondo fighter.

Since pads became a requirement of competition tournaments, their non-use in training studios has been linked to possible negligence claims. In practice, however, more injuries are sustained in tournaments that require padding than in those associated with controlled free sparring (*see* page 37). Initially, protective pads were used for competitive events only. Since their introduction into *dojangs*, it would seem that many taekwondo and karate students have forgotten the concept of controlled hitting — the force of their strikes and kicks has actually become more dangerous because they know the pads are there to protect them.

Sparring is a valuable tool, but is used much less in the training environment than it should be. Even the quality of sparring has suffered because studio officials have introduced excessive control measures to protect themselves from lawsuits.

It has been acknowledged that if contact sports are to continue as a legitimate recreational function in our society, those who run the training schools need to be adequately protected. The introduction of waivers — requiring taekwondo students (or parents of under-age students) to sign an indemnity form on entering a training school — are no longer unusual. Waivers have also become a prerequisite for students taking part in taekwondo tournaments.

Since bodily contact is an integral part of taekwondo training, it is important to realize that certain risks are involved. Training encompasses controlled sparring, throwing, the use of some weapons and breaking techniques. Although injuries are rare, they may occur. Possible injuries include contusions, falls, and occasionally broken bones. The elbow joint may suffer from over-extending the forearm (joint hyperextension), while muscle pulls are also fairly common.

Parents and students must not waive any deliberate attempt to injure. Similarly, injuries sustained on defective equipment or unsafe training devices would be due to negligence on the studio's part.

Signing a waiver once you have read, understood, and agreed with it, enables instructors to teach the techniques as they have always been taught. It also ensures that the training you receive is authentic and not a watered-down version. If you have chosen a reputable and legitimate studio, your training will take place in a safe, well-maintained facility.

Stances

In martial arts a proper stance is the foundation for everything you are going to learn. You may make many attempts before you succeed. Don't give up. As a beginner you will need to learn the six basic stances covered in this chapter, because they form the basis of everything you will be taught later.

opposite KICKS, PUNCHES AND LEAPS — THE TAEKWONDO ARSENAL.

⇨ **The ready stance**

The ready stance is a relaxed posture, yet it requires intense concentration. You will use this stance often in class because it is a very basic foundation and most drills and forms begin with it. You may also use this stance when you are preparing to defend yourself during class self-defence drills.

You assume the ready stance by bringing both fists up to your chin as you inhale deeply. As you fill your abdomen with air and expand your chest, step out sideways with your left foot. Your feet should be approximately shoulder-width distance apart. In that way, your stance is well-balanced with your weight placed evenly on both feet. While you step sideways, at the same time bring your fists down below your rib cage as you exhale. Then snap both fists out in front of you (to a height below your navel) with a quick, powerful movement so that they form a half circle at waist level. Your fists must not be too far apart.

⇦ **The horse stance**

This is a solid foundation stance commonly used in martial arts. It is very effective in training, especially when students are being taught to develop hand techniques. It is not a good stance for fighting, however, because it allows less manoeuvrability. The delay caused by getting out of a deep horse stance may force an opponent's advantage and runs contrary to strategy, tactics and penetrating techniques.

The horse stance begins with the feet together, both arms stretched out straight before you, and fists turned over so that the knuckles point upward. With your left foot step out wide to the side. Your feet are spread to about double the width of your shoulders, toes pointing forward. At the same time, snap your fists back to the waist while rotating them until the knuckles point down towards the floor. Ensure that the elbows are pulled in and the fists are resting against the bottom of the rib cage. Keep your back straight.

⇨ **The front stance**

This is another stance that is commonly used by all martial artists, as it provides a solid foundation from which to extend (step or move forward from a particular stance), or explode (leap forward from a specific stance into a technique). At the same time, the back foot supports a strong defence in stopping an attack.

Take a large step forward with your left or right leg, at the same time bending the knee perpendicular to the floor. Note that the depth of the forward step is about double that of a normal step. Check to ensure that your rear foot is kept as straight as possible, flat on the floor.

The knee of the front leg should be bent enough so that when you look down, the foot is obscured by your knee and is not visible. In the final position the feet should be shoulder-width apart to maintain stability. The rear knee is locked. Weight distribution is centred more strongly on the forward, bent leg.

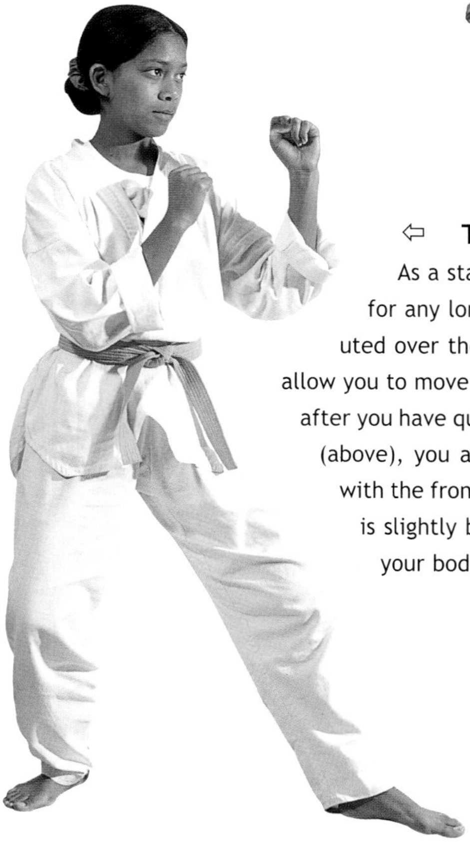

⇦ **The back stance**

As a stance that is defensive by nature, the back stance is not used for any long period of time. Since most of your body weight is distributed over the back leg, the main advantage of this stance is that it will allow you to move strongly and with determination in any direction you choose after you have quickly contemplated your next move. As with the front stance (above), you assume the back stance by first taking a large step forward with the front leg. This time, however, you ensure that your back leg, too, is slightly bent at the knee. The stance is correct when 75 per cent of your body weight has been shifted onto the back leg.

⇦ **The fighting stance**

It is imperative to learn this stance correctly because a bad fighting stance is an open invitation to anyone who is opposing you.

To get into a proper fighting stance, face forward with your hands clenched into fists and cross your arms approximately 15cm (6in) in front of your chest. (If you are right-handed, your hands should be crossed at the wrist with the right fist placed on top. Reverse this movement for a left-handed person.)

Take a step backward (roughly 50cm or 1½ft). Simultaneously snap the left hand back to the centre of the chest, while snapping the right hand forward approximately 30cm (1ft) in front of you. Note that the left hand is held close to the chest, knuckles facing up. It should always be centred on your chest, or it will be out of position for blocking and too slow to deliver an effective punch. Keep the left fist close to your chest, with the elbow of your leading hand (here the right) extended approximately 12–15cm (4–5in) from your body. In the fighting stance the feet should be shoulder-width apart, i.e. roughly 45cm (1½in) apart. The knees should be slightly bent and your body weight centred.

⇨ **The cat stance**

This specialty stance differs from other, more solid stances in that it allows front-foot action in a variety of front leg kicks without having to shift and redistribute your weight back and forth. The main benefit of the cat stance is the fact that weight does not shift; whenever a taekwondo practitioner has to shift to a new stance, he becomes vulnerable to an attack as his body weight is temporarily off-centre.

The cat stance is really a one-legged stance that is assumed by placing 95 per cent of your body weight on the back leg. The foot of your back leg is straight and flat on the floor. The front leg is kept slightly bent at the knee. Only the ball of your foot lightly touches the floor — ready to kick out at your opponent.

Fighting stance error

One of the most common mistakes beginners make is to turn their shoulders when stepping backward into the fighting stance. Do not turn too far sideways in an effort to lessen the target area presented by your body; ensure that you are facing to the front.

⇩   Standing with your body twisted so that you face your opponent sideways has two major disadvantages:

Rather than shield your body from attack, you expose your vulnerable side (where most attacks are targeted). Roundhouse kicks, the most widely used kicking technique during sparring matches, could be easily and effectively landed. It limits your arsenal of 'weapons'. From the side stance you cannot even reverse punch effectively without stepping.

Experienced fighters will know that from a side stance only four kicks can successfully be executed (among them are the side- and reverse kicks which generally do not require an adjustment of the feet). All these kicking techniques are difficult, however, and require much practice.

When you stand correctly, your weight is distributed in such a way that you will maintain your balance and can use effective kicking and punching techniques. Your kicks will be more powerful and have a better chance of reaching their intended target. Your opponent will know this and be alert to the danger.

⇩   When you stand in the open fighting stance you restrict your roundhouse target area and instead your opponent may attempt a front kick. If you are sparring against an experienced student: watch out. Most beginners, however, are unable to execute front kicks properly, tending to kick upward instead of inward. This means they invariably kick into a blocking elbow and the painful result is enough to dissuade them from making this mistake again. (For the correct way to execute front kicks *see* pages 62–63.)

The most important reason for using the open stance is that it enables you to apply every technique you possess without stepping first (and causing your opponent to move away because he is tipped off by your movement and knows what to expect).

Your safety zone

Whenever you are facing a hostile opponent, be it a sparring partner, or someone accosting you on the street, it is imperative to maintain your safety zone. Policemen use this tactic in the field.

The safety zone has to be a sufficient distance away from your opponent or opponents so that you are able to react appropriately should the need arise. As a rule, martial arts practitioners regard a good distance for a safety zone as being slightly further than the distance in which you can comfortably strike by extending your leg, i.e. about a step and a half.

Ensure that you are far enough away to force an aggressor to have to first move towards you before they can attack you. The safety distance will enable you to escape, or respond with a counter move.

A If you make the mistake of ignoring or neglecting to maintain your safety zone, you will stand too close to your opponent. You will be within easy range of each other, and the person who moves first or is the fastest will usually score first.

B Maintain your invisible safety zone and aim to stay out of range of your opponent's punches and kicks. In this way, natural ability and even experience is negated and both fighters are on a more equal footing. The step-and-a-half safety zone allows you to evade, block or counter whenever you choose.

Free sparring as a tool

Sparring is a very useful taekwondo tool that was developed primarily to give the student an opportunity to experience how hand and foot techniques should be delivered and blocked. Along with the use of his 'weapons' in sparring, namely the hands and feet, each student learns how to maintain a safe distance from the opponent, how to penetrate (safely invade someone else's safety zone), and how to effectively use strategy and timing.

As popular as sparring is in the training programmes of *dojangs*, it is important to understand that this is not always realistic fighting. Contact in sparring is usually light — students are taught to 'pull' or control their strikes so that they hit with minimal force, whether or not padding is worn. Furthermore, since instructors are at hand and closely monitor sparring sessions, strict rules are applied and the target areas are restricted. In a controlled bout, for example, no student may attack certain vulnerable target areas such as the neck, kidneys, spine, groin and back of the head.

Key components of many street fighting incidents (i.e. attacking the groin, throat and eyes) are strictly forbidden in free sparring, but are taught to advanced students as part of the taekwondo self-defence curriculum.

Speed and power in delivering techniques are instilled into the student's training regime through repetitive form practice and punching and kicking drills specifically designed for this purpose. Students learn the power of a striking hand or foot technique when they are taught breaking manoeuvres.

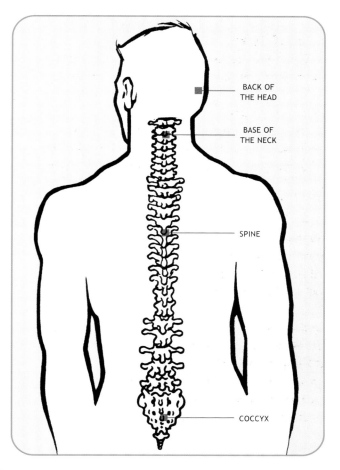

BACK OF THE HEAD

BASE OF THE NECK

SPINE

COCCYX

top WHEN YOU ARE FORCED TO DEFEND YOURSELF AGAINST AN ATTACKER, VULNERABLE BODY AREAS SUCH AS THE BACK OF THE HEAD, BASE OF THE NECK, SPINE AND SMALL OF THE BACK BECOME CHOICE TARGET AREAS FOR YOUR STRIKES, PUNCHES, KICKS AND CHOPS.

POWER, SPEED AND AGILITY — ESSENTIAL ELEMENTS OF TAEKWONDO.

ADVANCING IN SKILLS

One cannot go through life with only one set of keys. Wherever we start from, we can always find room to grow and change. So, too, in the martial arts. When an engineer builds a bridge he follows a blueprint, and if he follows the blueprint faithfully he ends up with a bridge. If another engineer picks up the same blueprint and follows it, he will have an identical bridge. That is the way of science. Art, however, is different. If a student is taught a curriculum leading him to a black belt and another person studies the same curriculum, the results will never be the same. That is the way of art.

Form training

Form training is the root and the true foundation of training in a martial art and should form an integral part of your taekwondo training routine. Many martial artists, even high ranking ones, do not know or understand forms. They may believe that, because they cannot fight with forms, they have no need for them. This attitude reveals a gap in their training.

Form training begins with very basic movements aimed at teaching the beginner how to step, turn, block and move. In some schools a student must perfect and practise a few dozen forms before he earns his black belt. As the student progresses, new forms are introduced which he must learn and practise. More advanced forms may teach students how to use their hips, how to turn with kicks and punches and how to effectively deflect blows from different directions. As students get more adept they may be taught how to incorporate leaping techniques, use sweeps and even execute takedowns.

According to traditional masters it takes three years to perfect one form. Many new students mistakenly believe that once they can 'walk through' a form properly they are ready to learn a new one. Not so. Experienced instructors know it takes years to develop anything of value. Probably the single most important benefit of form training is that it relies on repetition — one of taekwondo's best training tools.

Since different schools teach various sets of forms, a detailed discussion of forms in this beginner's guide would not be very helpful. For this reason only one typical basic example that beginners would encounter in their training has been highlighted.

Benefits of form training

As forms are learned they are practised over and over again so they become a physical notebook of the particular style the student is studying. Not only does form practice review the principles learned, it helps to perfect movement and technique. As a bonus, it is also an easy way to stay in shape.

Once students have mastered a particular form they can go through the movements alone whenever and wherever they please.

Form practice allows students to execute full-power kicking, blocking and punching techniques. It also focuses the mind to the exclusion of all else. By focusing exclusively on a form, students tend to become calm, which together with the ability to focus, are vital tools in self-defence.

In the martial arts there is always a starting place. The techniques that follow form the basic building blocks of taekwondo. Forms, punches, kicks and blocks are repeated — the idea is to make the student's reactions instinctive and automatic. No student should have to stop and think about what the next move is going to be. However, since strikes and blocks may be practised standing still or stepping, you first need to know how to step.

opposite ADVANCED STUDENTS WHO HAVE MASTERED THE BASIC PRINCIPLES OF TAEKWONDO ARE TAUGHT JUMPING MANOEUVRES.

Stepping

Learning traditional stepping is important. Some of the more modern martial arts taught today have slightly different stepping techniques, but lack the solid foundation of traditional stepping. Some teachers who have a different approach to that advocated by traditional methods teach the kind of stepping where you simply move forward as you would in normal walking. Incorrect stepping will cause you to lose momentum.

A Begin with a front stance. The right (back) leg is locked and the knee of the left (forward) leg bent.

B Now move the right leg forward towards the knee of the left leg. At this point, the knees should be bent and slightly apart, not together. Continue the forward movement with what was your back leg.

C As you execute the forward motion with your right leg you will notice that your weight shifts fully into your planted left knee. As your body moves forward, the planted knee will help to propel you, sending your weight and momentum forward along with your body, thus giving you greater power.

Some useful tips: What was the front leg (left) now becomes the back leg and is 'locked out'. The locked back knee is accomplished by a hip twist (this is imperative). When you add speed to this simple stepping principle of drive-momentum-twist, you achieve maximum power. Also, if you punch as you move, it creates a forceful blow. Be careful not to bend the back leg — it should be straight and locked. When each stance is completed the feet should be shoulder-width apart.

Hand techniques

Practising the moves

After the beginner student has learnt the basic hand techniques explained in this chapter, they are usually practised by doing each movement in rapid succession in sets of three, with a simultaneous Ki yap on the last strike. Such practice drills are commonly done in the horse stance.

For example: In the medium punch, after the first fist has struck it is retracted to its original belt position. At the same time, the other fist drives forward on the next count using exactly the same punching technique. As this fist reaches its target area, it is immediately and quickly retracted to its belt position while the other fist drives forward on the following count with the same punching technique. As the last — third — fist reaches its impact area, the puncher sounds a Ki yap. This drill can and should be used with all the hand techniques outlined in this chapter.

As each punch drives forward, the fist remains in a knuckle-down position until just before the impact. It is twisted over (knuckles up) on impact.

⇧ The medium punch

A Standing in a horse-stance position, place both fists thumbs upward at the waist immediately above the belt. First drive the right fist forward at solar plexus height directly ahead of the centre of your body. (In other words, your fist does not travel straight forward from the shoulder, but is aimed towards the opponent at an inward angle.)

B As the arm approaches 95 per cent of its extension, snap your fist over so knuckles are now facing up. (When stepping forward with the medium punch, the striking hand is immediately retracted to its belt position while the other fist strikes simultaneously.)

C The follow-up punch (i.e. with the other hand) is delivered with far greater force than the initial punch because of the 'equal and opposite' actions of the physics involved. The follow-up punch is executed by pulling back hard with the hand that has just punched, and punching with the other fist at the same time. Once you have thrown a punch, the hand is immediately snapped back to your belt at the hip level position.

⇩ The double punch

A The technique is exactly the same as it is for the single punch, but instead of executing the punches with each fist in turn and alternating, both fists now punch forward simultaneously.

B Turn both fists down at the last moment.

✶ The completed double punch shown here has an added snap. Just before the moment of impact, both wrists are rotated so that the fingers are now facing down and impact occurs with the top two knuckles (*see* page 28). Here, the left fist targets the opponent's chin, while the right fist is aimed at the solar plexus.

⇦ The high punch

A The high punch is done in the same way as the medium punch. The only difference between the two is that the imagined target area is now the opponent's head. The high punch is used for a clear shot at your opponent's head while avoiding his blocking or grasping hands and arms at the same time.

✶ In the completed high punch seen here, the fist is punching upward at an angle that is aimed at the opponent's head.

⇩ The spear hand

The spear hand uses exactly the same technique and momentum as the medium punch, with the exception that here — instead of a fist — all of the fingers are stiffly extended in preparation for the strike, and the thumb is tucked in along the palm.

A In the spear hand technique depicted here, note that the top finger is straight (as it always should be when using this technique) with the second and third fingers drawn back slightly so that all three fingers are in alignment. This is to avoid injury to the delicate finger bones by ensuring that impact is absorbed by all of the fingers simultaneously.

✳ Here, the spear hand is targeted for the throat of the opponent, a very vulnerable area.

Tip: Align the fingertips so that all fingers strike simultaneously at one moment of impact and absorb the shock together instead of separately.

THE OPEN HAND IS AN EFFECTIVE WEAPON IN DEFENCE AND ATTACK.

⇨ The double spear hand

The double spear hand technique is done exactly the same as a double punch, except of course that you use spear hands instead of fists. This is a useful counterattack movement, which can break through an opponent's attack easily and swiftly, while delivering a serious blow to his or her midriff.

A Extend the fingers while your hands are still close to the body. In the double spear hand, both hands are used as 'thrusting swords'.

B Drive your hands straight forward in a swift, powerful movement.

⇦ The forward knife-hand chop

This strike, which was originally known as the 'judo chop', is done with the hand in the open knife hand mode.

This is a devastating and powerful strike, which delivers the impact force through a relatively small area of the striking hand, thus increasing its force. A single chop is capable of easily snapping a collarbone, while a chop delivered to the back of an opponent's neck could be fatal.

A For a right-handed chop, bring the right hand back to the right ear.

B Retract the left hand to your side while the right knife hand simultaneously does a half circle strike to land in the opponent's temple area.

⇩ The palm heel

In the palm heel strike, a flat hand drives forward toward the opponent's chin, fingers opened but curled forward slightly so that they could impact with the opponent's eye area at the same time. Although this strike is aimed primarily at an opponent's chin, the powerful impact makes it a formidable weapon when it is directed anywhere to the facial area or directly to the chest or solar plexus.

A The forceful strike is aimed at the chin with the palm serving as the striking surface.

✳ A palm heel blow with the left, right blocks.

⇨ The knuckle fist

In this technique the fist is only half clenched so that your fingers rest on the pads at the base of the fingers. The fingers are not rolled any further to form a full fist. The knuckle fist technique reduces the size of the impact field, thus placing all the power of the strike into a much smaller impact area, which has the potential to cause much greater damage when aimed below the nose, or at the solar plexus or throat.

■ The thumb is tucked under the fist at the base of the curled fingers. Extend the second knuckle of your index and middle fingers and strike with these second knuckles leading (i.e. leading the hand in the striking motion). This causes the raised knuckles of your fingers to become the striking surface.

■ When the second set of knuckles is extended, the knuckle of the middle finger stands out slightly farther. This is what will make the initial impact. To support the raised knuckles and avoid injury, rest your thumb underneath the fingertips of the index and middle fingers.

⇦ The eye stab

This manoeuvre is a very basic yet effective striking technique. It is also invaluable as a self-defence weapon, as it can cause severe pain and momentary blindness.

A The eye stab is done with fist closed, except for the first two fingers. The index and middle fingers remain extended.

✳ The stab is executed with the first two fingers, as seen in this completed manoeuvre. A jab in the eye will disable your opponent and can cause temporary blindness.

⇩ The side chop

For an effective side chop the hand must be in the knife-hand position, but with palm facing downward.

A The arms are crossed over the front of the body. The uppermost arm and hand serve as striking weapon.

B The bottom arm returns to the side while the attacking hand simultaneously strikes in a flat arc.

✳ As you sweep the striking arm towards your target area and strike the opponent in a powerful flat arc, your other arm is retracted to the side of your body with a snap movement, hand closed into a fist. This lends the side chop technique the 'equal and opposite' balancing action that will result in an increase of the striking force.

⇩ The back fist

The back fist strike uses exactly the same principle as the side chop except that now, instead of a knife hand position, the hand is made into a tight fist with the little finger facing toward the ground and the index finger held topmost.

A The arms are crossed for 'equal and opposite' striking action. Note the vertical position of the fist which will allow the knuckles to make first contact.

B A fast snapping strike means you hit with the top of the knuckles instead of the front.

✳ A hit with the back fist to the temple or under the ear may disorientate your opponent. When it is aimed at the face it can make a crushing blow.

WARNING: When practising punching techniques never extend your arm fully. The punch should stop about 25mm (1in) short of maximum extension. Punching with your arm fully extended may cause hyperextension and damage the elbow.

⇧ The hammer fist

This strike is usually executed to the side in a swift and powerful forward-reaching motion. As before, the non-striking fist pulls back to the belt at hip level. At the same time, your striking arm is raised to a position vertical with the ground and continues with a forceful, outward-reaching strike.

A hammer fist blow to the nose will effectively end a fight, while a blow directed at your opponent's shoulder may cause his collarbone to fracture and could disable him.

A To accomplish the hammer fist technique, cross your arms over the front of your body for 'equal and opposite' striking action. The (left) striking arm and hand are held uppermost. Both fists are clenched.

B Look at your target and prepare to strike your opponent's head or upper body. Raise your left hand in front and slightly above your head.

C As you strike down with the left, the other hand (here the right) retracts to its position at waist level. The strike is accomplished with the bottom (hammer) part of your fist.

⇩ The side punch

The side punch begins when the fighter is in the ready stance position and ends in a horse stance.

A In a ready stance, with your fists pointing upward, you can execute the side punch.

B Take a step right towards your target. As you do so, the punching fist (here the right) remains stationary at its position just above but about 5cm (2in) forward of the hip. The other fist (here the left) moves straight across the front of the body and past the punching fist, palm facing downward. Look at your target as you rotate your upper body 90° (here to the right) in one fluid movement.

C Keep your feet firmly in place as you pivot into a horse stance. Shoot your right fist out straight to the side, twisting it palm down just before impact. At the same time retract the other fist to its correct position on your opposite side (at hip level). As you accomplish the punch, straighten your torso.

Tip: Pivot and punch simultaneously so that your body weight goes into the strike, not the floor.

Basic blocking techniques

Hand blocking techniques are most often practised while stepping forward. Drills, on the other hand, can be done while moving forward and backward using a different block with each step. Note that hand the techniques are also often practised using a different one with each step.

⇩ **The low block**

The low block is performed with the outside lower edge of the blocking arm (here in a horse stance).

A This manoeuvre is done by bringing the fist (here the right) across your body and up to the opposite (left) shoulder while positioning the left fist to protect your groin area.

B Now use the blocking right fist to fire downward from the shoulder and across the body to the outside edge of your right knee. It should end up one fist-height above the knee.

C The right fist has just completed the right low block and the left fist has retracted to the hip position at the same time.

✳ Here, the fighter on the right used a right low block to successfully deflect a left front kick that was aimed at her stomach area.

⇧ The high block

An easy way to understand the high block concept is to imagine that your blocking fist grabs hold of a knife and is then fired upward as if you were trying to puncture a balloon hanging above your head.

A Start in the ready drill-position, arms braced at your sides, hands clenched into fists, knuckles down.

B Now cross the arms over the front of your body in preparation. (The blocking arm's fist should end near the opposite armpit, knuckles pointing out).

C As you pull the non-blocking arm backward by bringing the fist to the belt position, allow the block-ing arm to sweep up and outward, turning the fist over as the arm moves up. The arm stops raised above your head, elbow angled to deflect a downward blow from your opponent. Note that the blocking arm uses a forceful striking motion, NOT a mere limp lift.

✳ You will use the high block often as it can intercept most strikes to your face.

⇧ The outside block

The purpose of an outside block is to intercept blows aimed to your middle so the block must be fast, hard and determined to intercept and deflect the attack.

A Perform this block by first crossing both arms in front of your body, hands closed in fists, with the blocking arm (here the right) at the bottom.

B Retract the top or non-blocking arm to the side to stop with the fist at belt level. Simultaneously, move the blocking arm outward with the elbow bent at 90°.

C In the final position, your fist stops just to the outside of the shoulder.

✳ The outside block is effective in intercepting and deflecting punches aimed at your middle, as seen in this manoeuvre. You can also practise this effective blocking manoeuvre while stepping forward or backward.

⇩ The inside block

The inside block is an intercepting manoeuvre to deflect an opponent's blow or kick. It can also be called a deflecting block.

A To perform this block, assume the starting drill-position, fists braced against the sides of your body.

B Bring the non-blocking arm parallel to the ground across the front of your body. At the same time draw the fist of the (left) blocking arm back to your ear.

C Now pull the non-blocking arm swiftly backward, bringing this fist to the belt position. At the same time fire the blocking fist with a twisting motion across the front of your body. Be sure to maintain a natural bend in your arm so that the fist strikes, palm upward, at shoulder height — just to the outside edge of your opposite shoulder.

✱ At the moment of impact, twist the fist sharply to face palm upward and snap it backward a short distance. Note that the block is made with the inside part of the forearm.

⇩ **The reinforced block**

The reinforced block uses exactly the same method and technique as the outside block, with the exception that this time the non-blocking fist does not get drawn back to rest at the customary waist position. Instead, it accompanies the blocking arm and reinforces it at impact time by supporting it at about elbow height.

A Assume the starting drill-position.

B Swing your right arm outward from the opposite side to execute an outside block and follow this with the left fist, pressing it against your blocking arm for additional support.

C With this reinforced defensive position you are ready to block an oncoming kick.

✳ A strong, reinforced block (seen in this completed manoeuvre) can be used to effectively stop and deflect a kick from your opponent.

⇧ The double chopping block

The double chopping block is a very quick and versatile blocking technique that can successfully be done from most stances. One hand blocks an attacker's punch while the other hand comes back to the centre of the chest, preparing to deliver a follow-up strike or block, as the situation demands.

A Both hands should be in the open knife hand position. In this case, the right hand is in front, ready to block the opponent's attack, while the left is held palm-up in an on-guard position close to the chest.

B Bring both hands back and up behind your left shoulder. The right hand should stop at the ear, palm facing towards your face. Extend your back hand slightly further out with the palm facing away from you. This is the ready position.

C Next, sweep the right arm outward (exactly as you would in an outside block) with the hand still remaining in the knife hand position. Turn the hand as it travels so that the outside knife edge of the hand becomes the striking surface. Note that the arm is bent at the elbow as it is in the outside block. Remember to tuck your thumb in to prevent injury. This also helps to tighten the striking surface of your hand. As you strike

with the front hand, simultaneously bring the left arm forward so that the knife hand stops at the chest, palm up. The chop block with the right deflects a punch, while your left hand in a knife hand position on your chest, as seen in the sequence above, ensures that it is ready to strike or block next.

✱ In this completed sequence the opponent's right middle punch was successfully deflected with a left chopping block. Here, the right knife is seen in an on-guard position on the chest, ready for further action.

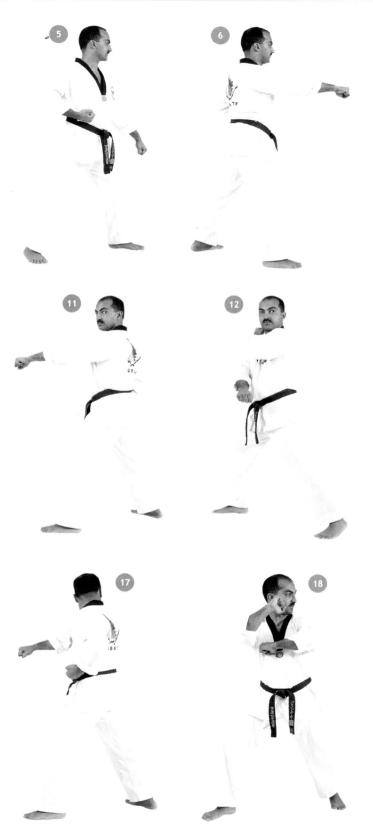

Form training (*Hyung* or *Poomse*)

Hyung or *Poomse* are Korean for form training, an important element of all martial arts. Each form consists of offensive and defensive movements and employs a series of coordinated steps, punches, blocks, kicks and strikes that have been systematically combined. The World Taekwondo Federation (WTF) standardized a set of forms called *Taegeuk Poomse*. The following example is of the **Taeguek One (*Il jang*) Hyung**.

1–3. Bow in the attention stance (feet together); move left foot into ready-stance position. Place both hands in front of abdomen; move them up in front of your chest and down again just below belt level; fists should be be about one fist distance away from body.

4. Look left; move left foot 90° left; raise left arm for low block; right hand protects groin area.

5. Left forward stance; downward block with left.

6. Step forward with right leg into walking stance; execute right punch to middle.

7. Start looking towards rear.

8. Slide right foot backwards diagonally (final position is 180° from 5.); position arms ready for right low block.

9. Complete turn; low block with right arm.

10. Step into left forward stance; execute left front punch to middle.

11. Look left (to front).

12. Start left hand block while beginning left turn by pivoting on ball of right foot.

13. Move left foot into extended forward stance; simultaneously execute left low block.

14. Follow with right reverse punch to middle.

15. Step into right forward stance with right foot by pivoting on ball of left; simultaneously execute left reverse inside middle block.

16. Move left foot forward assuming left forward stance; right reverse front punch to middle.

17. Start looking towards rear.

18. Slide left foot backwards diagonally (final position is 180° from 15.); position arms ready for middle block.

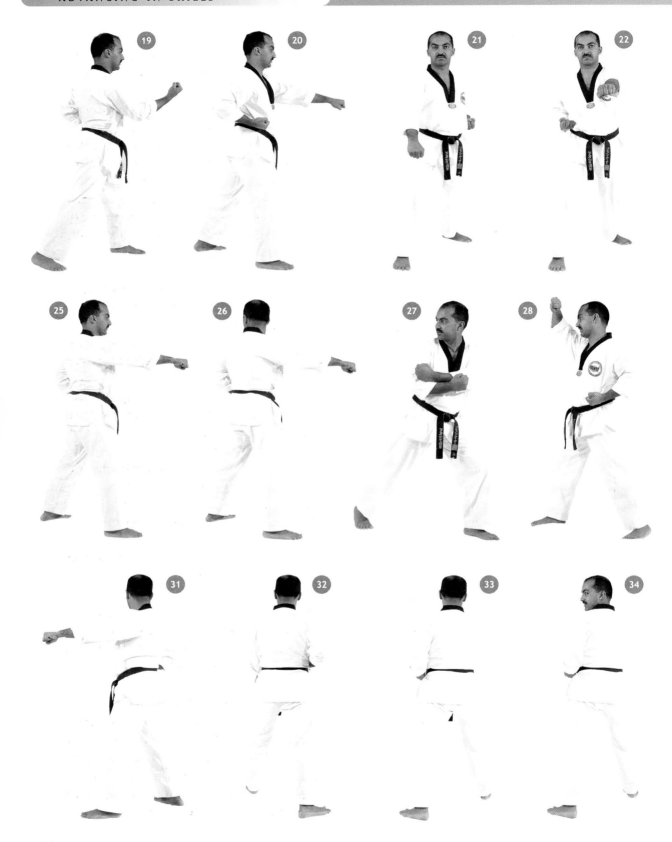

19. Turn left by pivoting on ball of right foot; move left foot into left forward stance; execute right reverse inside middle block.

20. Step forward with right foot into right forward stance; left reverse front punch to middle.

21. Pivot on ball of left foot to turn right and step forward with right foot into right extended forward stance; execute right low block.

22. Execute left reverse front punch to middle.

23. Step slightly forward and left with left foot by pivoting on ball of right into right forward stance; simultaneously execute left head block.

24. Execute right front kick.

25. Assume right forward stance by dropping right foot forward; right front punch to middle.

26. Start looking towards rear.

27. Slide right foot backwards diagonally (final position is 180° from 25.) and position arms ready for high block.

28. Pivot on ball of left to assume right forward stance; turn body at completion of movement and execute right head block.

29. Execute left front kick.

30. Drop left foot forward assuming left forward stance; execute left front punch to middle.

31. Look right.

32. Assume left forward stance (pivot on ball of right, place left forward); left low block (see 13.).

33. Step forward right into right forward stance; Ki yap and right front punch to middle (see 25.).

34. Look to left rear (front).

35. Pivot on ball of right, turning counterclockwise to face in original starting direction.

36. Bring left foot next to right foot, assuming ready stance and bow to finish.

Considerations for Poomse

The two main aspects of form practice are physical and mental attitude. The first refers to how a student performs (endurance, strength, speed and balance), while the mental aspect concerns the student's state of mind. Both aspects should be perfectly balanced for maximum benefit.

KICKS AND BREAKS

Taekwondo is primarily a kicking art. Unhampered by the rules that govern traditional martial arts, the Koreans have had the freedom to repeatedly revise, refine and improve various kicking moves until their efforts resulted in potent and highly effective techniques.

Basic kicking techniques

Before beginners can move on to the many flying, hopping and jumping penetrating manoeuvres that are performed by advanced taekwondo students, they must learn basic kicking. The basic kicks are not unlike those done in karate, but slight variations make the Korean versions more adaptable for advanced techniques.

The kicks outlined in this chapter are the foundation stones of taekwondo. They need to be practised until the student grasps the speed, snap and drive of each kick and is thoroughly familiar with the positions and proper placement of the feet. Different situations require different kicking techniques, such as snap and power impact, thrust and speed.

While learning basic kicking the beginner is first taught 'in place' kicking techniques that cover his front, back and the sides of his body. Not only will the student learn how to use the back or front foot in various basic kicks, he will also be shown the correct foot placement and delivery of the kick, as well as the necessary stances and weight shifts. Most importantly, the student will be taught the use of knees and hips to deliver kicks swiftly, accurately and effectively.

Once the basics have been acquired, the techniques are ingrained through constant drilling until they become natural and are executed with ease. It is only at this point that the teacher can move ahead and teach the student how to apply the techniques while stepping forward, backward and to the side, how to use kicks while jumping and hopping in any direction, and finally, how to use kicks while flying through the air. Once students have learnt these techniques, they must learn how to apply them in combat situations they will encounter. In other words, students will be taught what each kick is designed to do and precisely when to use it.

There are many training devices and drills that aid in the teaching of these techniques. These are kicking bags (both stationary and swinging), hand-held paddles, body-braced kicking pads and bar jumping drills.

Master the basics

Before any beginner can move on to learn advanced drills, he needs to study and practise the very basics. Without the proper hip twist, foot turn and correct foot positioning, any kicking technique will be useless.

For example, without a well-executed knee lift, the front kick will be ineffective and would easily be blocked by an opponent; unless a side kick is issued from its proper beginning position, it can be jammed; and an incorrectly executed roundhouse kick can leave the kicker dangerously off balance and vulnerable to a counter-attack by the opponent.

To be a good kicker and a taekwondo champion — either in form or in a fighting competition — it is necessary to learn the basic kicks that your instructor assigns to you and practise them repeatedly.

Always remember that nothing good comes easily. Do not become discouraged if this part of your training requires much improvement. Keep practising and, after a while, you will wonder why you were ever concerned about it. Naturally, your instructor should have a solidly based foundation in traditional Korean martial art. Only if he knows the correct mechanics, can he build his students into formidable kicking opponents.

opposite IN THIS TOURNAMENT PICTURE, A KICK FROM RED CLASHES WITH A SPINNING JUMPING KICK LAUNCHED BY THE OPPONENT.

⇩ The front snap kick

The front snap kick can aptly be described as one of the anchor techniques of taekwondo. While it is practised often, inexperienced fighters seldom use it as it takes a painful period of trial and error to learn the effective and correct way of delivery.

Usually the first kicking technique a new student learns, the front snap kick — not surprisingly — is often discarded almost immediately, because it can be extremely painful to the kicker when delivered incorrectly. Do persevere: it is an awesome weapon when it is used correctly.

The most common problem inexperienced kickers encounter lies in the fact that they are taught to kick upward instead of inward. This causes the top of the kicker's foot to connect with the opponent's elbow. The ensuing pain is often severe enough to discourage the kicker from trying to apply the technique again. A high knee lift is the key to making the front snap kick effective and painless.

A Assume the cat stance by shifting your weight onto the back leg to free up your front kicking leg.

B Bring your right leg up and raise the knee higher than your belt. Then quickly unhinge the kick inward — like a punch — to drive it underneath your opponent's guard and straight in towards the unprotected middle area of his body.

C Flick your lower leg up.

✳ Remember to kick forward and pull your toes back so that contact is made with the ball of your foot to deliver a powerful clubbing smash right on target.

⇧ The front thrust kick

The front thrust kick is primed in the same way as the front snap kick, using a high knee lift. However, at the point where the knee is lifted high, instead of unleashing a snapping kick from the knee that bangs into the target like a punch, the kicking foot is thrust inward like a spear. The power behind this kick is produced by a strong thrusting drive of the hips. By leaning the body slightly backward, the ball of the foot is driven forward in a piercing type of thrust rather than a power punch.

A The front thrust kick is done with the back leg.

B Lift your knee (here the right) higher than your belt to ensure that your kick will penetrate below your opponent's guard.

C Use a driving hip motion and a slight backward lean to thrust the foot forward like a spear.

✳ A landed front thrust kick will leave your opponent winded and may damage his ribcage.

⇧ The roundhouse kick — back leg

This kick has different names, but is most commonly known as 'roundhouse' because of the upward half circle described by the kicking foot. The back leg roundhouse kick is like a cannon-blast hook punch — it hits hard and is very difficult to avoid even if you can see it coming.

A Start by raising back leg (here the right). Raise the heel of the kicking foot behind your back as if you were kicking yourself in the buttocks.

B Next, pivot immediately towards your opponent with your right shoulder and right knee pointing at the target area.

C Loosen the knee joint to 'unhinge' your raised lower leg and slam it into the target. This movement should be executed in one smooth, continuous motion.

✳ Two different foot positions can be used to deliver the impact of a roundhouse kick. When the ball of the foot is used as the main striking surface it delivers a

blow very similar to a punch; if the instep is used, however, the result is a heavy, clubbing type of strike. If you were at the receiving end, you would clearly feel the difference between the two.

⇩ **The roundhouse kick — front leg**

The front leg roundhouse may not hit quite as hard as its back leg counterpart, but is sneaky as it travels, lightning fast, only a short distance before it reaches impact point.

A Cock your hips by dropping your hipbone towards the back leg which carries your body's full weight. This will allow you to perform the front leg roundhouse kick, even when you are standing in close proximity to your opponent.

B The front leg roundhouse kick, too, is best accomplished by raising the knee of your front leg slightly, as though you were assuming the front kicking position. Then comes the slight twist of the hip, and you slam your foot forward in a circular and nearly horizontal motion towards its target.

C The foot impacts either with the instep or the ball of the foot just as it would if you were executing a back leg roundhouse kick.

✱ From a proper fighting distance (i.e. by observing your safety zone — *see* page 36), the technique is used much like a boxer's jab would be and is very effective when your target stands close to you.

By rotating the hip of your kicking leg so that it is cocked upward, you effectively drop the opposite hip so that it is lower. If you are close to your opponent you cannot hope to execute the kick successfully unless you cock your hips and kick up. It is harder to deliver a roundhouse kick when you are positioned close to your opponent as you must kick up in order to ensure success, but it can be done.

⇧ The 'in step' kick

There are two different basic methods taught for this kicking technique which is also called the 'in crescent kick'. In both, your kicking foot swings outward and upward to clear your opponent's elbow and shoulder.

A The in step is not a good technique when you are standing too close to your opponent and are jammed in by the proximity of your target. Bend the standing leg (left) slightly at the knee as you raise your right foot for the first part of the kick.

B & C Now your foot circles up and over the elbow and shoulder to club the opponent's head.

✳ Aim to land the kick in the head area with either the inside edge of your foot or the sole; both are good hitting surfaces. As your foot approaches the target, finish the kick by snapping your foot at the target to complete the manoeuvre.

⇩ The 'out step' kick

The out step, or out crescent kick is done with the back leg. It is the same as the in step, only to the other side.

A In this technique, your weapon is the outer edge of the foot, which becomes the striking area. Here you start with the foot positioned some way to the left.

B & C Next the foot travels first to the left and then moves quickly upward before coming back to the right to strike the target. The out step kick is a winner when you are in close proximity to your opponent.

✳ In this completed out step kick, you have closed in on your opponent and he is jamming you to the front with his bulk positioned more to one side of your body. The benefit of the out step kick manoeuvre is that you are still able to use the outside edge of your foot to deliver a kick to the target.

⇩ The side kick

The side kick is an essential taekwondo technique and should form part of every student's arsenal. Not only is it a great offensive weapon, it also provides invaluable defence. Unfortunately, although it looks very easy, it is probably the most abused and imperfectly performed of all kicking techniques.

There are numerous types of side kicks that are used in a variety of different situations. In learning the basics, the taekwondo student is taught both the front leg side kick and the rear leg side kick. The obvious difference is that the front leg version is launched while standing in place, while the rear leg side kick is delivered with a pivot, bringing the back leg to the front and then thrusting it forward.

Both kicks are accomplished by slightly pivoting on one foot while bringing the kicking leg up to knee height. At the same time the knee of the standing leg is bent so that your stance is lowered by around 2cm (almost one inch). This manoeuvre causes the lower part of the kicking leg to stay retracted, but places it in a position parallel to the ground. The knee-lowering motion cocks the hips, in readiness for the swift thrusting motion of the kick.

A Lowering the standing knee (here the left) causes the lower part of the leg to stay retracted and parallel to the ground. The cocked hip drives the right leg with the body weight behind it.

✳ Whether as an offensive or a defensive weapon, the side kick is absolutely essential. A quick retraction step keeps it always available. Remember that the outside knife edge of the foot is the contact area.

Tip: Make the outside edge of your foot a proper weapon by ensuring that it is in the correct position. It should be turned downward on impact.

Common side kicking errors

Once you master the basic side kick you can use it while sliding, hopping or jumping forward or backward. Eventually you will even be taught how to incorporate it into flying leaps. Before any such advanced skills can be taught and understood, however, mastering the basics is your prime goal. Here are a few tips to help you in perfecting your side kick technique.

A Instead of lifting both the knee and the foot as required, the kicker lifts only his knee, leaving his lower leg dangling. The resulting kick will be upward and inward, instead of directly inward. This weak technique is easily blocked.

B This kicker's movement is exaggerated, he leans back and sideways too much and could lose his balance. The knee is off centre, the kick will be off target.

The bonus of a correctly executed side kick is that it will enable you to drive an attacker backwards. If you continue to practise the technique, you will perfect your side kick and find that no one can successfully invade your safety zone.

Consider, however, that some fighters will charge right back at you after getting kicked. To counteract this you will need to learn how to 'reload' your side kick by quickly dropping the ball of your kicking foot to the floor to regain balance and momentum, then bouncing it right back up again. Ensure that your leg (from knee to foot) is parallel with the floor at all times so that you are ready to fire out again, and again if need be.

Prime target areas for side kicks are the neck, the side of the body, abdomen, ribs and knee joints. As with most kicks, look at your opponent when delivering this attack. Avoid letting your upper body lean too far down as this can unbalance you and diminish the power of your kick. Keep your hands in an on-guard position. This way you will avoid letting them fly about wildly.

⇦ The reverse kick

The basic reverse kick is taught from a fighting stance. In this sequence the stance is demonstrated starting with the left leg and left shoulder forward.

A From a ready stance, twist the torso backward by pivoting on the ball of the front foot and the heel of the back foot so that your stance is again shoulder-width apart. Turn the head at the same time and look at the target over your right shoulder. Now bring the heel of the right leg (now the front leg), straight upward until the lower portion of the leg is parallel to the floor and the heel is pointing at the target.

B With a quick backward spin, thrust the right kicking leg forward until it locks at the knee. Your ankle should also be locked, so that the toes point down as much as possible. The knife edge or heel of the foot becomes the striking weapon.

C In a normal fighting stance you would be facing into your opponent's arm and hand defences. The quick pivot and reverse kick of this technique brings your foot into contact with a less defended target area.

The torque generated by the quick twisting turn makes this a devastatingly powerful kick. Like most taekwondo kicks, it can be done with a sliding, hopping or jumping motion, either backwards or forwards.

⇧ The double jump kick

This kick can be done while flying forward, jumping backward or standing in place. The most useful of the three is the flying-forward double-jump kick, which is always done while airborne with neither foot touching the floor. The technique is especially useful for 'stealing' distance, i.e. when you are too far away from your opponent and need to get closer. It employs an initial kick and a follow-up kick and uses two striking options — the front-snap and the thrust kick. You begin by driving forward as if you were going to run at your opponent, precisely the move you would like him to think you are going to make. Now extend the leg below the driving knee into a front snap kick. This results in your opponent stepping away into safety. In the second half of the manoeuvre, kick forward with your back leg and

drive it at the target while still in midair. The follow-up kick (also called a hitch-kick), extends your attack area right into your opponent's safety zone. He cannot step back far enough to escape.

A & B From your initial fighting stance lift the knee of the driving leg (here the left) as if you were going to run at your opponent in order to decrease the distance between you. This will force him to employ an evasive tactic to move back and out of your reach.

C Complete the initial kick with your right leg while you are airborne.

D Then follows the second kick (here a hitch kick with the left), which also drives forward while still airborne. This leg drives forward into the opponent's target area with the full force and momentum of the attacker's body behind it.

The art of breaking

Prior to 1980, protective pads were rarely used during sparring bouts in taekwondo training. Full-speed and full-power strikes, punches or kicks administered with the hands or feet were forbidden. Sparring occurred between opponents wearing no padding whatsoever, whether the moves were offensive or defensive. Bare knuckles and unclad feet were the weapons of the day and, unlike modern sparring, the face was a prime target. Yet, injuries were rare and heavy contact was even rarer due to the extreme control taught by the masters, and practised and observed by the students. Even beginner students were expected to be able to swat a fly off someone's nose, leaving the nose untouched. At that time, a true measure of the power behind a martial arts blow had to be determined by breaking techniques.

Between 1940 and 1945, martial arts training was focused primarily on fighting for one's life, either with bare hands or weapons. Striking a training partner was taboo. It may seem paradoxical, but students were not taught superb control. Instead they learnt that they only had one chance: one kick, one punch, or one throw. If these were ineffective, they did not survive.

Every move had to be decisive, each opponent had to be rendered harmless. If an enemy could survive what the martial artist considered to be his best effort, then it meant that the martial artist would be unable to survive on the street.

In today's modern taekwondo schools, the breaking of inanimate objects such as wood, glass, brick, a block, or rocks is still used during testing periods to measure a student's breaking ability, and thereby power and technique. Some students view breaking as an ultimate art in itself; they will always aspire to add just one more board or brick in an attempt to surpass their previous achievement.

It is customary for breaking tests to be administered when students are about to advance in rank to a superior belt level. No good instructor will expect his students to perform breaking techniques that are beyond their individual capabilities. Breaking tests are not a test of courage, instead they provide a measure of the student's skill and confidence.

Heavy breaking techniques (also known as fancy breaking) are usually studied separately and apart from the normal curriculum. This advanced type of breaking is most often used when schools perform demonstrations. The requirements aim to assess the power that students are able to generate, as well as the calmness and confidence they display at that particular stage of their training.

There is no substitute for the serene approach and calmness of mind that allow you to look your attacker squarely in the eye and then deliver a strike to your chosen target without flinching. Great confidence is what every martial artist must have, and breaking is one of the tools instructors use to instil it in their students. Confidence will compel a student to do what is necessary and effective, without hesitation.

THE HANDS OF THOSE WHO HOLD THE WOODEN BOARD SHOULD GRASP THE EDGES FIRMLY TO PRESENT A STABLE SURFACE.

Breaking materials

The most common breaking materials used to test beginners are at least four or five pieces of 2-grade, white pine wood. The wood should measure at least 30x30cm (12x12in) and have a thickness of 2.5cm (1in). Ensuring that the boards are properly and securely held is essential for the execution of a successful breaking manoeuvre and to avoid unnecessary injury. The instructor is responsible for making sure that all requirements are adhered to.

Testing procedures

Students who are still undergoing basic training will not be required to break items with the knuckles of their fists. Fist punching requires conditioning that is only expected of advanced students. The breaking performance required at beginner's level will most likely entail a downward chop, hammer fist or a side kick.

The sequences on the following pages demonstrate different breaking techniques as performed by a right-handed student.

THE PEOPLE HOLDING THE BOARD MUST STAND ABSOLUTELY STILL; ANY SLIGHT MOVEMENT COULD SPELL INJURY FOR ALL CONCERNED.

⇧ The hammer fist break

A In this break, one board (there may also be two, depending on the student's ability) is suspended between two upright cement blocks. (Stand with the shoulder of your striking hand positioned directly over the item that is to be struck.)

Tip: Establish correct stance position by placing your fist on the board before executing the break.

B Place your left foot up close to the left-hand cement block, bending the knee slightly. Place your right foot further back, leg straight. Now roll the hand into a tight fist, thumb tucked in to prevent injury, and raise it up and back as high as possible while twisting the hips left. Next, the left non-striking fist moves up and approaches the right shoulder, while your eyes are kept focused on the board.

C Sound a Ki yap as you begin to drive your right fist in a powerful downward blow towards the floor, ignoring the board you are about to break.

Once the material is properly placed, intense focus, concentration and confidence as well as follow-through are elements that will ensure your success in demolishing the boards effectively.

Try to drop your body weight into the strike. To do it correctly, bend your knee as your fist descends with its bottom edge as hitting surface.

⇩ The downward chop

The stance in this break is identical to the stance used in the hammer fist break. In this break, however, when you raise your arm, your striking hand is not clenched into a fist; instead you use the knife hand position.

The next key move is achieved by rotating the striking hand while the arm is raised, with the thumb tucked as far inward to the palm as it will go. This ensures that the hand descends in the proper mode and will avoid unnecessary injury.

A Initially the right arm is raised to full extension. The striking hand is in the knife hand position with the thumb tucked securely into the palm of the hand.

B Now rotate the wrist backwards to ensure that contact is made with the proper hitting surface.

C Ki yap as you bend your knee (here the left) and strike for the floor. Drop your body weight into the breaking motion when your fist descends. Together with speed and confidence, the strike is made. The muscle pad of your hand makes the contact, similar to a palm heel strike.

> **Tip:** In a downward chop, the strike is not made with the entire edge of your knife hand. Slide your finger along the edge of your hand from the base of your little finger. You'll feel a bone near your wrist. Directly in front of it is a muscle pad. This is what serves as the hitting surface.

⇩ The side kick break

In this break it is important to keep your eyes and mind focused on the board that you are going to break. From a fighting stance (*see* page 34) step forward to execute a side kick (*see* page 68). Ensure that the heel of your kicking foot is pointed right at the target. While doing this, turn your hips towards the board you intend to break and drive your kicking foot towards it in a smooth but powerful motion, using the momentum of your weight as you drive forward.

In this photograph the person holding the board has remained immobile, but turned his head sideways to protect his face. Note where the board was originally held (x), which indicates the effective penetration that can be accomplished.

Note: Under no circumstances should any beginner experiment with breaking techniques unless he or she is undergoing appropriate conditioning training under the expert guidance of a master. Incorrectly executed breaking manoeuvres can cause serious and lasting damage to hands and feet.

SPORT AND SELF-DEFENCE

Sport taekwondo is a puzzling phenomenon. While free sparring is widely used in studio training to teach discipline and build character — sparring with strangers outside the studio flies in the face of the Asian cultures where most martial arts originated.

Martial arts that are taught as self-defence regimens invariably begin by teaching students defensive blocking techniques before they go on to striking manoeuvres. As this concept is quite contrary to almost all open tournament competition, where the focus is on aggressiveness, it is surprising that masters and grand masters have not banned sport taekwondo.

In the past, most Asian men avoided competition, with the exception of some great martial arts teachers who would take up challenges to improve their livelihood. In years gone by, oriental schools held yearly championships within their own styles to determine reigning champions. Today, however, these championships have made way for prize money, celebrity status and advancing a school's reputation. Many martial arts schools not only attend open tournament competitions but also host them.

Different categories

Sport taekwondo falls into two vastly different categories, namely point fighting (originally executed with bare hands and controlled to a certain degree) and the Olympic-style full-contact sparring with pads as dictated by the World Taekwondo Federation.

Relocation of Korean taekwondo instructors and grand masters to other countries around the world took place primarily between 1960–70. In practising a form of taekwondo that had only recently evolved from Japanese karate, early competitive taekwondo events featured point fighting similar to that seen in karate.

Travelling to various countries, the masters settled in cities and towns with sufficient population numbers to support the schools they intended to establish. As their art developed and their reputations as martial artists grew, so did the ambition and inquisitiveness of their students anxious to test their new-found prowess.

How tournaments started

Tournaments were the obvious answer and masters met with fellow masters in nearby locations to set up events in an effort to oblige their students' wishes to compete. Initially, competitive events consisted mainly of invitational contests against neighbouring schools or *kwans* that practised the same style of taekwondo. Later, as tournament competitions began to blossom, the areas expanded and the masters began working and cooperating with each other until, eventually, a tournament circuit had been established.

This system entailed the mailing of invitations to participating schools within the circuit to attend a tournament in one of the circuit cities. By changing the venues throughout the year, each master was given the opportunity to host his own tournament. As competition grew, individuals with outstanding talent emerged in the finals or as champions. These would move into other circuit areas to test their skills against new opponents. This led to super tournaments and the naming of national champions in the art.

The growing tournament trend brought with it a noticeable change in the nature of tournament fighters. Also, insurance companies began to insist on the use of protective sponge-rubber armour or padding for all tournament competitors even in non full-contact competitions. Taekwondo experts agree and practical experience has shown that the wearing of padding or armour does not necessarily make the sport safer as it diminishes the fighter's control, yet the rule stands.

opposite SELF-DEFENCE MANOEUVRES RELY ON COURAGE AND SPEED. PRACTISE THEM UNTIL YOU ARE CONFIDENT.

Tournament format

For a beginner it is useful to know what to expect when taking part in a taekwondo tournament, as it can be quite a daunting experience until you become accustomed to competing against other students.

Most circuit tournaments are held in high-school gymnasiums where there are usually eight competition rings. A ring measures roughly $6m^2$ (65 sq ft), but may sometimes be a little smaller, and has two scratch or starting marks on the floor.

Although contestants are expected to arrive early, tournaments rarely start on time. The event usually begins with a short introductory programme that serves to introduce the visiting masters and explain the tournament rules. Black-belt students attending the tournament are the first to conduct their form competition since they also act as referees and judges.

Next, ring assignments are announced over a public address system, indicating where the black belts need to report to fulfil their judging and refereeing functions. This is followed by programme announcements informing participants involved in different *gup* or belt division competitions. Let us follow the contestants through a typical tournament:

In all divisions, form competitions are always the first event to be held in a ring. After presenting their registration papers to the ring attendant in charge, contestants await their turn with their fellow participants. Five form judges are seated at the far end of each ring, with the senior judge usually occupying the centre seat.

The ring scorekeeper announces the participation sequence of contestants in the match and then calls the names of those 'on deck' — those who will compete after the match that is in progress has been concluded. As each individual's name is called, he or she stands before the judges and bows. In some tournaments, competitors are required to state their name, school and the form they are taking part in. After a competitor has bowed to the judges he commences the form, then turns his back as the scorekeeper tallies the judge's scores, before bowing again and leaving the ring.

TO SIGNAL THE END OF A MATCH THE REFEREE CALLS *KO MAWN* AND EXTENDS HIS RIGHT ARM IN FRONT OF HIS CHEST, HAND IN A KNIFE HAND POSITION.

Once the adult form competitions are concluded, the score keeper carefully tallies the five judges' scores. Usually, each contestant's highest and lowest scores are discarded, the first to prevent favouritism and second to eliminate prejudice. The remaining three are added and the highest score determines the winner. If form competitors achieve a tie, the judges will request a repeat of their performance, either together or separately. When the first three place winners have been determined, they are called forward to receive their trophies or medals.

Fighting spirit

After the form competition is completed in a specific ring, the sparring competition takes place. Divisions are usually kept in the same ring for both form and sparring events.

All competitors hand in their sparring competition papers and are lined up with other competitors in their level and placed in line according to height and size. When a tournament is divided into different weight categories (heavy-, middle- and lightweight), a competition is held independently for each different weight division. A champion is named in each of the categories — these champions compete against each other for the title of grand champion.

Once all the fighters have been paired they are entered onto a bracket sheet (a line-up of tournament matches), after which they are called into the ring. When the names of a pair of competitors are called, they step forward. Judges are positioned with either a red or blue flag in each corner of the ring, while the ring referee stands in the centre. The referee's first task is to initiate the bowing of the competitors and to set them into the fighting position with the command 'Free fighting position, Jun be!' The referee also controls the match and is one of the officials scoring the match. At the referee's next command, 'Fight' or 'Go', the match begins and competitors start sparring with each other in an attempt to score points.

Bouts last three minutes for all levels and the winner is the fighter who scores the most points in this period. Winners advance on the bracket sheet, while the losers

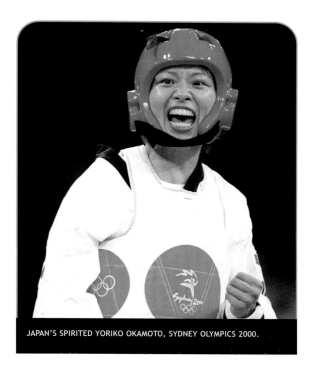

JAPAN'S SPIRITED YORIKO OKAMOTO, SYDNEY OLYMPICS 2000.

are dismissed. This rule applies specifically to single-elimination contests. In pool-system competitions the losers get another opportunity.

Adhering to rules

Tournament rules are very strict. One reason is, of course, to ensure the safety of all present, another is to enforce discipline. Competitors are not allowed to talk back to officials or dispute their rulings. While fighters are allowed to contest the judges' decisions, they may not do so personally — it has to be done by their instructors.

Beginners may not face-punch or kick below the belt. Back-fist attacks (hitting with the back of the fist) and blind attacks (spinning strikes in which the person doing the technique does not first look to see where the strike is going) are not allowed.

Fighters are also forbidden the use of open-hand techniques or ground attacks (attacking while an opponent is on the ground). When a corner judge or referee sees a point being scored he shouts: 'Point'. The match is stopped and the referee calls for confirmation, at which time all flags are raised simultaneously to avoid judges trying to imitate the others' scores.

A TITANIC CLASH BETWEEN JORDAN'S MOHAMED ALFARARJEH (RIGHT) AND GERMANY'S FAISSAL EBNOUTALIB DURING THE SYDNEY OLYMPICS IN 2000.

Judges indicate points scored by using their red or blue flags in different ways. One of the fighters wears a red chest protector: when he scores the judge will indicate that a point has been won by waving a red flag. If the judge has failed to see a point supposedly scored, he holds the flag horizontally across his eyes, indicating that he did not see it. If he disagrees that the technique earned a valid score, he waves the flag back and forth at ground level.

When it comes to scoring points, the majority rules. Only those judges who see the point being scored are counted. The point is only allocated if there is a majority count. After three minutes the timekeeper stops the match, points are tallied and the winner progresses to the next bracket. A 'bye' system is usually used and worked into the brackets to ensure that matches end correctly. In the last series of matches four competitors compete against each other; the two winners go on to the finals while the two losers compete against each other to determine third place.

After the final match the winners are rewarded and competitors either leave with a trophy, or a desire to do better next time.

Olympic contests

Beginners rarely compete in Olympic taekwondo matches as these are reserved for black belts only. Olympic-style competitions are conducted with the competitors wearing full armour or padding which consists of a torso-covering vest, helmet, as well as protective hand and foot coverings.

The International Olympic Committee (IOC) sets the rules for Olympic competitions — it has adopted these from the World Taekwondo Federation. Face-punching in Olympic-style fighting is forbidden by the IOC.

Students are, however, permitted to combine any kicks with full-power strikes to the head (strikes meant to be knockout blows, whose force is not controlled). In Olympic competitions all techniques are delivered at full power. Any technique that produces a 'trembling shock' scores a point (this term denotes a full-power strike that leaves the victim too shocked to retaliate). Matches may also be won by knockout.

Four judges preside and a referee controls the match. The judges and the referee keep score cards, which are checked and tallied by other masters to determine the overall winner.

Self-defence

Almost everything that is done in a taekwondo *dojang* focuses on self-defence, or Ho shin sul (the 'protect-body art'). Form practice, sparring, breaking and the entire philosophy of the taekwondo style of martial art taught in the studio are an integral and ongoing part of self-defence training. The activities are meant to place the participants under stress, and teach them how to cope with that stress. This, in essence, is the way of taekwondo.

The entire approach of taekwondo would be lacking, however, if it did not include the hands-on aspect as a culmination of all the other activities. The hands-on approach to self-defence differs from the stress of standing in a ring to fight someone who outweighs you by 23kg (51lb). It teaches students how to escape from those who mean them harm, how to throw them, escape their grabs, sweep them off their feet and use pressure points to inflict pain and force their attackers to release them. In a *dojang*, these techniques are often introduced under the guise of *Hapkido* and most of them are derived from the Korean police art called *Do su bang oh*.

Self-defence needs to be practised with a partner in a non-threatening environment. The manoeuvres are dangerous — they entail strikes to the eyes, throat, groin and joints. Training allows the participants to take on the roles of aggressor and victim in turn and thus realize what damage the techniques can cause.

Groups of students are taught prearranged and set self-defence sequences. Although this method is somewhat unrealistic and artificial, it allows them to master the techniques. It also helps them to understand how effective they are when applied correctly.

Taekwondo schools have different approaches. In some, black belts graduate with very little knowledge of actual self-defence, while others are much more self-defence oriented and teach it as part of their curriculum. In such a school, students would learn around 20 new self-defence series at every belt testing level. By the time these students attain their black belts they would know over 200 highly effective self-defence moves that can be applied in almost any situation.

Self-defence training will cover many different threat elements such as hand- and wrist-grabbing, belt-grabbing, neck-grabbing, knife attacks and choking. No matter what, taekwondo students will also learn that very few of the techniques they are taught can be effective unless they manage to punch, kick or head-butt an attacker first in order to make him release his grasp.

The sheer number of self-defence techniques taught by masters in taekwondo *dojangs* worldwide, and the countless variations that exist, make it impossible to incorporate more than a token few that can be considered representative of the kind of training a student of taekwondo can expect. The following are five essential basic training routines.

THE AIM OF SELF-DEFENCE TRAINING IS TO EQUIP YOU TO HANDLE DANGEROUS ENCOUNTERS AND SURVIVE.

Repetition is essential in self-defence training

Occasionally, aerobic schools and fitness centres offer self-defence classes, but it is questionable how much these institutions have to offer in the way of solid, serious training, and how much use the student will derive from attending the courses they offer.

To become an instinctive reaction, and one that is useful when you need it most, self-defence training must be practical and structured. It must include basic blocking and striking techniques and needs to be practised repeatedly and regularly until the techniques become ingrained and second nature.

It is also important that techniques are practised with sufficient force and determination so that both the person doing the technique and the practice partner will understand what they are learning, how it works and how effective it can be.

In most cases there will be some form of physical contact between aggressor and victim — be it that an attacker has hold of your wrist, clutched his hands around your neck or has grabbed a handful of your hair.

⇧ **Escape from a wrist-grab**

A An attacker has grabbed hold of your left wrist.

B Weaken his hold on you by jerking your hand up towards your shoulder, at the same time twisting it in towards the attacker's thumb. This action is usually done with a quick jerk, but a slow, steady pull will accomplish the same results.

C Twist your arm forward and out to loosen his hold on your wrist, always moving against his thumb.

D Once you have escaped the wrist grab, continue lifting your left hand until it is in line with your right ear. You are now in a position to counterattack.

E The offensive reaction depicted here is a back chop strike that will land a sharp knife hand blow across the attacker's ear. You can follow this up with another punch or a kick if necessary.

Tip: Kick, punch or strike out to repel an attacker's grip before you use a self-defence technique.

Note: Self-defence requires you to use your head. Rather than jumping at the opportunity to apply what you have been taught in the *dojang*, your main aim should be to act sensibly and responsibly. Avoid danger, possible conflict and self-defence situations at all cost. A few common-sense rules always apply: don't venture into areas you don't know, or belong in, especially on your own; keep doors locked when you are travelling in your car; avoid dark doorways and alleys when you are walking in unfamiliar territory. If you suspect that you are being followed, don't be afraid to run. Screaming 'fire' is bound to attract more attention than if you were to yell 'help'. Find a well-lit area, or shop. If there are inhabited houses nearby don't hesitate to pound on doors.

If you have no other option: face your opponent bravely and with determination. Make it clear that you are angry and will not be victimized.

⇩ The s-bar

A An attacker has grabbed your right wrist. You will use your free (left) hand to trap his grasping hand by immobilizing it or holding it in place.

B Place your left hand over the attacker's wrist to hold it in place for your next manoeuvre.

C In one quick movement rotate your right wrist, palm towards your body, until you can move your hand up and over the attacker's wrist. Do this while keeping his hand trapped with your left placed firmly on top of it. Place the knife edge of your hand (here the right) across the forearm bone of your attacker's arm. Remember to keep his hand straight in line with his forearm. Press down quickly and with unrelenting force, leaning your body weight down into the knife-edge press as you do so.

D This locks the attacker's wrist, causing him excruciating pain, and will force him to his knees. You now have him at your mercy and can follow up with a kick to his groin or a knee strike to his solar plexus or head.

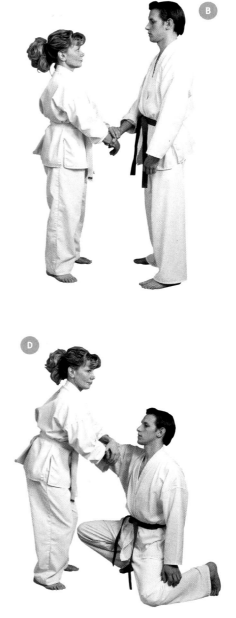

⇩ The shin banger

The shin banger is a simple yet effective technique that should cause sufficient pain to debilitate your attacker, thus allowing you time to escape. In some cases you may feel it appropriate to follow up with an elbow strike. Remember: he who fights and runs away lives to fight another day.

A You are confronted on the street by someone who obviously means you no good. Don't be afraid, but look your opponent straight in the eye.

B Your attacker reaches for you with both hands. Block him, by inserting your lower arms between his, forcing them apart and releasing his hold on you. As you do this, grasp his sleeves or arms with a strong grip. Hold on and pull him closer to you.

C As you pull the attacker towards you, drive the instep of your foot or shoe straight into his shin, making sure that you do so with a straight forward slam, not a circular motion, as that would diminish its effectiveness. Hip action will increase the force of the blow.

Legal aspects of self-defence

Remember that the action you take to defend yourself may have costly consequences. Any time you strike or kick someone else you could open yourself to legal action, especially if you do a good job on your attacker. Legal concepts regarding self-defence vary throughout the world.

You need to be aware of how it is defined in your country, as your definition may not coincide with that of the law. You need know how and when it may be used — what you may do to protect yourself and what is not permitted.

In the USA, for example, one concept states that deadly force in self-defence is only allowed when a person is in fear of death or great bodily harm. The individual does not necessarily have to be correct in that assumption, as long as he or she thinks and truly believes it in their own mind. Once the victim no longer fears for his or her life, the defensive behaviour should cease immediately, or they would become the aggressor, thereby forfeiting their right to self-defence (i.e. if you have neutralized your attacker and he is lying on the ground, do not give him an extra kick for good measure).

⇩ The rear neck-hold

A An attacker grabs you from behind, his right arm is around your neck in a tight strangle hold.

B Step right and aim a reverse elbow strike into his stomach with your left arm. This will wind the attacker and force him to release his hold on you.

C Quickly step back, placing your left leg behind his right, and aim a determined punch at his face or neck area. The punching action will make him rear backwards, but since your leg is already in position, he will lose balance and fall, thus preventing further attack and allowing you to escape.

⇩ **The shoulder grab from the side**

A An attacker grabs your shoulder from the side using his left arm.

B Swing your right arm over and back around his arm, locking his elbow in the process. The lock will force his body backwards, while the grip itself causes great pain and could also break the arm.

C Quickly step to your right, moving slightly behind his left foot and aim a knife hand strike (*see* page 44) to his throat.

⇩ **The roundhouse hook-punch attack**

This is a simple but effective sequence that will enable you to take down an attacker. The technique relies on speed and the surprise element, and must be practised until you know exactly what to do without having to think about it first.

Remember that you are in close proximity to your attacker throughout this manoeuvre — if you fumble or are unsure about the next step in the sequence you place yourself in more danger. Unless you act quickly, with firm determination and authority, an attacker could find ways to retaliate.

A An attacker swipes at your face with a right round-house hook punch, also referred to as a 'haymaker'.

B Defend yourself with an open-hand high block with the left hand (the open hand generally moves faster than the fist). Then strike at his face with a high right punch while maintaining a secure grip on his right arm with your blocking hand.

C Open the hand of your punching arm, which is still near his face, and grab and pull his neck forward while pushing his right arm down with your left hand. This technique will cause his body to come forward and towards you. Exploit his proximity by kicking him with your knee (here the right).

D Immediately swing your kicking leg behind his back leg without putting your foot down and pull forward to sweep your attacker's legs out from under him. Simultaneously strike his chin with a palm heel strike (*see* page 45), stabbing your fingers in his eyes at the same time, for greater effect.

E This should cause the attacker to fall. As he does so, lock his body by pushing your left knee into his left elbow and maintain your grip on his arm. In doing this, you are forcing his body into a very vulnerable position onto its side. This will prevent him from using either his legs or his left hand to launch a counterattack at you from the ground.

F Pivot onto the ball of your right foot and execute a knee strike by dropping down onto his hip or lower rib cage. Simultaneously punch him in the chest. Once he is incapacitated, you can make your escape.

GLOSSARY

AIZU	The referees' gestures and signals	HYUNG	(also known as Poomse) A form, or traditional sequence of steps used as training device.
AH HOOL	Nine in Korean		
AP CHAGGI	Front kick technique		
AP KI PUN CHAGGI	Front thrust kick technique		
		IL GOOP	Seven in Korean
CHAWBI	(also known as Taiken) A Chinese martial art combining the arts of kenpo and jujutsu	ITF	The International Taekwondo Federation, a private art-sport organization founded by Gen Choi Hong Hi specifically for followers of his Taekwondo style.
CHAW CHOOM SAWGE	Horse stance		
CHA YANG CHA	Turn left		
CHA YOO TAE RYUN	Free sparring, friendly fighting under supervision	JUN BE	The ready-stance position
CHO NAYKI	Outside block technique	JUNG DAWN CHI LU KI	A medium punch
CHO NOKI	Inside block technique		
CHUN GUL SAWGE	Front stance position	KARATE	Okinawan/Japanese fighting art
CHAW REYAWT	Position of attention	KAE SOK	An order to continue
		KI YAP	The shout, yell, or bark that is exhaled on contact.
DA SAT	Five in Korean		
DOBOK	Taekwondo uniform	KO MAWN	Finish, return to beginning stance.
DOJANG	The training hall, or studio	KONG SU DO	(empty hands) A fighting art
DUL	Two in Korean	KWAN	School, or organization, teaching a specific style of Taekwondo.
DU SU BONG	Korean police art		
		KWAN BUP	Chinese boxing art
FOCUS	The skill of bringing body weight, strike, concentration and the ki yap together at the crucial moment of impact	MASTER	A learned teacher of martial arts; never less than a fourth degree black belt.
GRAND MASTER	A learned senior instructor whose students are themselves master instructors. Grand masters have attained the rank of seventh-degree black belt or higher.	NET	Four in Korean
		PAAH DO	Ridge-hand (a strike with the top edge of the hand)
GUP	Korean word for step, indicating the training level of a student.	SAWGE	Stance
		SAW BAWM NIM	Instructor
		SET	Three in Korean
HANA	One in Korean	SHOTOKAN	A Japanese style of karate promoted by Gichin Funakoshi.
HA DAWN MAWKI	A low block		
HOOK DE	Black belt — the belt itself	SHUDOKAN	A Japanese style of karate promoted by Toyama Kan Ken.
HO SHIN SUL	The art of self defense		

GLOSSARY

SI JAWK	Command to begin	WAIVER	Legal document acknowledging the risks that may be involved when participating in a certain sport or function, and agreeing to go ahead despite of these risks.
SONG DAWN CHI LU KI	High punch technique		
SONG DAWN MAWKI	High block technique		
SOO DO CHIGI	Chop with bottom edge of hand		
SPARRING	Controlled fighting bout		
		WTF	World Taekwondo Federation; private body approved by Korean government; controls full-contact use of the sport in the Olympics.
TAEKWONDO	(hand-foot way) Korean fighting art		
TAE RYUN CHAW SAWGE	The fighting stance		
TAE SU DO	(kick-fist way) Korean fighting art		
TI RO TOE RA	Turn around	YA SAT	Korean for six
TOE RA	Turn	YA DUL	Korean for eight
TOL YOH CHAGGI	Roundhouse kicking technique	YOO DAN JAW	Black belt — the person
TUI CHAGGI	Back kick technique executed while facing front	YUL	Korean for ten
		YUP CHI LU KI	Side punch technique
TUI TOL YOH CHAGGI	Reverse kick technique, executed on turning	YUP CHAGGI	Side kick technique

Note: The Publishers have noticed major discrepancies in terminology and spelling of moves, stances and various other taekwondo terms. We are, therefore, aware that the terms printed here may differ from other sources.

PHOTOGRAPHIC CREDITS

All photography by James Evans (pages 22, 24, 27, 41, 44, 47, 48, 53, 55, 68, 69, 74, 76, 84, 85, 86) and Nicholas Aldridge, with the exception of those supplied by the following photographers and/or agencies (copyright rests with these individuals and/or their agencies):

4–5	Corbis	25	Sporting Images
8	Rob Young	31	Empics
9	Corbis	37	Rob Young
10	Rob Young	39	Rob Young
12	Rob Young	43	Rob Young
13	Mohamed Jaffer	61	Empics
20	Corbis	81	Empics
23	Tony Stone Images/Gallo Images	82	Empics

The publishers thank all the models who participated in the sequences depicted in this book.

USEFUL CONTACTS

INTERNATIONAL TAEKWONDO ORGANIZATIONS

There is no universal governing body to unite Taekwondo organizations worldwide. Some people belong to one or several organizations, others to none. Most organizations are self-serving, controlling only those who belong to them. They do not represent schools or kwans, which are probably the largest Taekwondo group in the world.

AUSTRALIA
- INTERNATIONAL TAEKWONDO FEDERATION AUSTRALIA
- 1/5 BROADMEADOWS ROAD
- MAROOCHYDORE
- QLD 4558 (Queensland)
- E-mail: muleta@itftaekwondo.com
- Website: www.itftaekwondo.com

AUSTRIA
- INTERNATIONAL TAEKWONDO FEDERATION AUSTRIA
- Wimberger Gasse 8
- 1210 Vienna
- Tel: (+1) 522 13 86
- E-mail: itf.austria@chello.at
- Website: www.itf-austria.at/

BELGIUM
- INTERNATIONAL TAEKWONDO FEDERATION BELGIUM
- Kasteeldreef 39
- 9890 Gavere
- Tel: (+9) 384 61 28
- E-mail: taekwondo1@pandora.be
- Website: www.itf-taekwondo.com

CANADA
- CANADIAN TAEKWONDO FEDERATION INTERNATIONAL
- Tel: (+306) 525 0005
- Fax: (+306) 525 0050
- E-mail: mailto:ctfi@sk.sympatico.ca
- Website: www.ctfi.org

DENMARK
- DANSK TAEKWONDO FORBUND
- Postboks 9
- 6870 Olgod
- Tel: (+75) 24 62 50
- Fax: (+75) 24 62 51
- E-mail: sekretariatet@taekwondo.dk
- Website: www.taekwondo.dk

GERMANY
- DEUTSCHE TAEKWONDO UNION E.V.
- Luisenstraße 3, 90762 Fürth
- Tel: (+911) 974 8888
- Fax: (+911) 974 8890
- Website: www.dtu.de

- INTERNATIONALE TAEKWONDO FEDERATION DEUTSCHLAND E.V.
- Malvenweg 27
- D-51061 Köln 80
- (Hohenhaus)
- Tel: (+221) 636 95 18
- Fax: (+221) 636 78 63

ITALY
- TAEKWONDO FEDERATION ITALY
- Via Massiego 40
- 31032 Casale sul Siele (TV)
- Tel/Fax: (+422) 82 26 02
- E-mail: fitae_segreteria@hotmail.com4
- Website: www.taekwondo-fitae0itf.com

MALAYSIA
- MALAYSIAN NTERNATIONAL TAEKWONDO FEDERATION (MITF)
- Lot 221, 2nd Floor, Jalan Sungai Hilir, 93150 Kuching, Sarawak
- Tel: (+82) 23 13 68
- E-mail: sta@ace.cdc.abu.com
- Website: //hope.cdc.com.my

NETHERLANDS
- INTERNATIONAL TAEKWONDO FEDERATION NETHERLANDS
- Teunisbloem 4
- 5754 SB Deurne
- E-mail: coos@wanadoo.nl
- Website: //itfnederland.cjb.net

NEW ZEALAND
- INTERNATIONAL TAEKWONDO FEDERATION NEW ZEALAND
- BOX 457
- Silverdale
- Auckland 1462
- Tel/Fax: (+9) 426 6696
- E-mail: secretary@itfnz.org.nz
- Website: //itfnz.org.nz/

NORWAY
- GLOBAL TAEKWONDO NORWAY
- Postboks 1129, Nyborg, 7420 Trondheim
- Tel: (+73) 88 31 90
- E-mail: info@gtf.no
- Website: www.gtf-taekwondo-do.no

INTERNATIONAL TAEKWONDO ORGANIZATIONS

SOUTH AFRICA
- **SOUTH AFRICAN NATIONAL TAEKWONDO FEDERATION**
- P.O. Box 117
- Retreat 7965
- Tel/Fax: (+21) 701 1701
- E-mail: ashihara@iafrica.com
- Website: sataekwondo.8m.com

SOUTH KOREA
- **WORLD TAEKWONDO FEDERATION**
- 635 Yuksam-Dong, Kangnam-gu
- Seoul 135-080
- Tel: (+2) 566 3505
- Fax: (+2) 533 4728
- E-mail: wtftkd@elim.net
- Website: //myhome.elim.net/ taekwondo//

- **KOREA TAEKWONDO ASSOCIATION**
- Olympic Park, 88-2 Oryun-Dong, Songpa-gu, Seoul 135-080
- Tel: (+2) 420 4271
- Fax: (+2) 420 4274
- Website: www.koreataekwondo.org

SPAIN
- **FEDERACION ESPAÑOLA DE TAEKWON-DO TRADICIONAL**
- Calle Mercado No. 3
- Benidorm, ■ Alicante
- Tel/Fax: (+96) 585 98 55
- E-mail: fefu@ctv.es
- Website: www.ctv.es/USERS/ fefu/festt/festt.html

SWEDEN
- **SWEDISH INTERNATIONAL TAEKWONDO FEDERATION**
- Box 92026, 54102 Skövde
- Tel/Fax: (+500) 42 71 68
- Website: www.itfsweden.com

UK
- **ACTION INTERNATIONAL MARTIAL ARTS ASSOCIATION (AIMAA UK)**
- 17 Bridgewater Park Drive
- Skellow, Doncaster,
- S Yorkshire, DN6 8RL
- Tel: (+1302) 33 0012

- **BRITISH ISLES TAEKWONDO FEDERATION (BITF)**
- Cathburn Road, West Lothian
- Morningside
- Lanarkshire
- ML2 9QO, Scotland
- Tel: (+169) 838 1753

- **UK TAEKWONDO ASSOCIATION**
- P.O. Box 162
- Orpington
- BR6 0WU
- E-mail: headoffice@ukta.com
- Website: www.ukta.com

USA
- **ACTION INTERNATIONAL MARTIAL ARTS ASSOCIATION**
- 4217 San Mateo Boulevard
- NE Albuquerque
- NM 87110 (New Mexico)
- Tel: (+505) 881 1888
- E-mail: aimaahq@aol.com
- Website: www.aimaa.com

- **AMATEUR ATHLETIC UNION TAEKWONDO (AAU)**
- National Headquarters
- The Walt Disney World Resort,
- Box 10 000, Lake Buena Vista
- Orlando,
- FL 32830-1000 (Florida)
- Tel: (+407) 934 7200
- Fax: (+407) 934 7242
- Website: www.aautaekwondo.org

- **AMERICAN TAEKWONDO FEDERATION (ATA)**
- ATA National Headquarters
- 6210 Baseline Road
- Little Rock
- AR 72219 (Arkansas)
- Tel: (+501) 568 2821
- E-mail: atausal@aristotle.net
- Website: www.ataonline.com

- **KOREAMERICA TAEKWONDO UNION (KARU-ITF)**
- 441 South Main Street 97
- Manchester
- CT 06040 (Connecticut)
- Tel: (+719) 578 4632
- Fax: (+719) 578 4642
- E-mail: USTUTKD1@aol.com
- Website: www.ustu.com

- **UNITED STATES TAEKWONDO UNION (USTU)**
- One Olympic Plaza, Suite 104C,
- Colorado Springs
- CO 80909 (Colorado)
- Tel: (+719) 578 4632
- Fax: (+719) 578 4642
- E-mail: USTUTKD1@aol.com
- Website: www.ustu.com